Stori

FISHERS OF MEN

STORIES TOWARDS AN AUTOBIOGRAPHY

GWYN A. WILLIAMS

First Impression—May 1996

ISBN 1 85092 335 5

© Siân Lloyd

Printed in Wales at
Gomer Press, Llandysul, Dyfed.

CONTENTS

FOREWORD

1985. A quiet restaurant in Johannesburg. A hurriedly arranged end-of-shoot party. There were seven of us: five liberal white South Africans, Gwyn, and I. We had just completed five days of unnervingly furtive filming on crowded and uneasy street corners, in parks where blacks were suddenly being rounded up and bundled willy-nilly into heavy vans with slits for windows, and outside imposing government buildings—under the magnificent African sun, and behind the backs of an ugly regime. Our 'undercover mission' accomplished, we were looking forward to going home. The informal get-together was a time to relax with our small film crew, new friends whom we had never previously met and whom we would never see again. It had been a new experience for Gwyn and for me—flying to a foreign location to work with people we didn't know but in whom we had to put our trust. It was after all an uncomfortable country to be in. We were two very nervous Welshmen —both somewhat lacking in physical stature—when, on our arrival in the country, we crept up to the immigration desk at the airport to be confronted by a seven-foot Afrikaaner in a peaked cap who might have been Corbus Wieser's older brother.

'You go first,' said Gwyn. 'You're taller than I am, and you don't stammer.'

I was an inch or two taller, but I had my doubts about the stammer in such a sweat-inducing situation. Flying into Cardiff Wales Airport had never been like this. But we both got through unscathed; our lying had been brazen if not profound. I had said that I was writing a book about Eisteddfodau in the far-flung outposts of the former British Empire, and Gwyn pulled his Dowlais wool over the officer's cold steely eyes by explaining to him that he was researching the worldwide Cymric diaspora, which the Boer giant probably thought was some newly discovered disease of the bowels. However, we got into the country, and we hugged one another like little kids.

But now, it was time to start thinking about leaving. We didn't do that until the following day, the day of our departure. There were better things to do at the end-of-shoot party; good food to be eaten, good wine to be drunk, and good company to be enjoyed. For the first hour or so there were small conversations between two or three at this end of the table, between two at the other end, and between another two across the centre: the sound recordist was a friend of Winnie Mandela and wished there had been time for us to go to Soweto, the runner thought that Breytenbach was more essential reading than Coetzee, the director talked about Grierson and Documentary, etc., etc., etc. And then, when we got to the dessert—which was soon forgotten—there were no more disparate chats. Why was the dessert forgotten? Why did the disconnected fragments of conversation gradually peter out? One reason only. We were listening to Gwyn, and we were all hoooked. I don't remember exactly what he was talking about; we'd consumed a lot of wine. But I seem to recall that it had something to do with the break-up of Tito's Yugoslavia, which hadn't yet, of course, happened. And there were also some prophetic points being made about South Africa and its foreseeable, or unforeseeable, future. Whatever the matter, the one thing I remember clearly is Gwyn's 'gift of the gab' and his spellbound, feed-me-till-I-want-no-more, dumbstruck, captive audience.

I was reminded of that solo-voice symposium when I read, in 'Welsh and a Social Disease', those words of the terrified Griffie on the way to Llangrannog— 'You know more than I do . . . You talk, I'll smile.' And that is what happens when we read *Fishers of Men*. Gwyn talks, we smile. In fact, we do more than just smile; we chuckle and we laugh. And the author would be perfectly happy with that. He himself probably chuckled a lot when he was writing them.

We shall all remember Gwyn A Williams, the People's Remembrancer; we admired his scholarship, we were enthralled by his books, and didn't know quite what to make of his powerful television persona except to agree that he was certainly different and that he made history entertaining. But in this, sadly posthumous, collection of autobiographical pieces we find Gwyn Alf the Rememberer. This is the 'five foot and a fart Mam's boy' from Dowlais reminiscing about his childhood, the frantic and frightening falling-over-oneself discovery of an explosive puberty, and his hilarious and equally poignant war experiences as a young nineteen-year-old soldier who knew the 'Deathless Splendour' and the 'Ineffable Glory of Being Welsh'! He says somewhere in his book 'I felt then, as I've felt many times since, particularly in southern France, that I'd been born in the wrong place.' Thank God that he was born in Dowlais!

I was privileged to work with Gwyn on a handful of television productions. I am told on good authority that I was chosen to act as Gwyn's Welsh language adviser because we had certain things in common: we were both short, we both smoked too much, and we were both iron and steel boys from the South Wales valleys. That is why we got on pretty well together. I only wish he'd been allowed time to write more stories towards his autobiography. There was so much to remember. So much more talking to do. We could have gone on listening for a long, long time—as we did in Johannesburg in 1985. There was a lot of smiling to do. Sadly, we were deprived . . .

Dafydd Rowlands

9

FISHERS OF MEN

We were a Gwernllwyn Chapel Gang. The Chapel was totally Welsh and we were committed to its many rituals—Sunday School, Young People's Fellowship, Trips to vulgar Barry Island and respectable Porthcawl and Pontsarn the Beautiful, the sports, the eisteddfodau, the Christmas parties—and the world premieres of my uncle Leyshon's Welsh plays for the BBC in the Schoolroom!

But our language was English. I suppose I was better equipped than most since I took Welsh as a secondary subject up to Matric, the then equivalent of O level. But my parents, Welsh-speaking themselves, never taught me the language. I think they assumed I'd absorb it by osmosis. Welsh became to us a Chapel tongue, a sacerdotal language.

War and the threat of war dominated our English-speaking adolescence. We'd spend hours passing and swapping cigarette cards of warplanes, warships, tanks up in the gallery where we always sat, while the preacher's voice in his sonorous Welsh cascaded around us. We'd stare fixedly at Japanese Zeros and American Flying Fortresses, with rather more alarm at German Messerschmidts and Heinkels. Why were ours always such awful old biplanes?! I remember the huge relief when the cards began to register Spitfires and Hurricanes! But still . . . why didn't they have cannon?

We became expert in all things military—which led on to me acquiring vast quantities of scale model warships and tanks which I'd deploy on the kitchen table. After War actually broke out, maps became an obsession and led on onto the first table top War Games.

We all met in our kitchen. I realise now that it was because we had more room and our family lived on the princely five-pounds-a-week teacher's salary. My mother, who'd been a teacher herself, used to test us all in General Knowledge quizzes, with much shuffling of paper and pencils and furrowing of brows. One question sticks in the mind still—'How big is the Swiss navy?' This we found a real stinker. It never figured on any cigarette card! In the end, Davy

William entered 'Moderate'. 'Ah! David William!' quoth Mam, 'you're going to be a civil servant!' He did, too.

Davy William (on no account was he to be called Dai Will, his mother would throw tantrums) was one of the inner gang. A very tidy boy, respectable—*decha* in our street Welsh—he used to display surprisingly tigerish qualities at times. There was Davy Blackwell, a square, solid figure, soccer and rugby player, not given to many words but faithful. He and Davy William lived next door to each other in North Street, in contrasting would-be petty-bourgeois and resolutely working-class homes. Then there was the enigma Glyn Harris, whose mother kept a shop over by Dowlais Church. His sister Glenys, who had one squiffy eye, was the constant companion of Joan Owen, the love of my life. Glyn took advantage of this, with a style, a suave insouciance and a kind of sniggering innuendo which enraged me. Seemingly much older in manner than the rest of us, he cultivated an offhand and cynical manner which used to drive me crazy. Perhaps because he tried to slope me with Joan Owen! Despite this permanent tension between us, he persisted.

There were a few stray bods as well but my real mate was Griffie James. His parents ran a great gaunt pub, the Bush, down by the tram terminus. I used to go into it, down a long corridor which smelt permanently of beer into their little kitchen. His father I never saw. His mother was very kind but seemed racy, smoking and drinking! She used to turn up in Chapel occasionally, causing a sensation. I think she was trying to civilise Griffie.

He was Mam's favourite. Very intelligent, he and I shared the honour of coming Third in the Borough during entrance exams into secondary school! He was lively, anxious and eager to please, but quick to frustrated rage. He was obsessed with technology and we called him The Engineer. He was to become a very skilled one, too. He used to wave complex diagrams in front of our bewildered faces, flourish his pencil and shout—'Can't you see, you ignorant slobs? It's a kind of piston arrangement!'

In those late thirties, we all succumbed to science-fiction. The local paper shop, known as Luvvie's because of the owner's customary greeting, was full of magazines. I used to case the joint for the gang.

She once claimed I read every magazine in the shop before buying one. I couldn't have done; no time! But we settled on *Amazing and Astounding Tales of Science Fiction*, with the absolutely stunning new worlds they opened up. Today I understand these magazines are Classics, housing some of the finest writing by the first practitioners. I certainly know all their names. But at that time, they were unspeakable anathema. Every time there was a noise at the door, there'd be a mad scramble to secrete them under cushions or anywhere to hide them from the gaze of stern fathers.

But with this endlessly interrupted inspiration, the Gang settled to the job of producing *Our Own Magazine*. I was made Keeper of the Records. And what records they were! We'd scribble away endlessly, each to his taste: my fantastic tales of new worlds, Glyn's attempts at adult cynicism, Griffie's unquenchable innovation.

Griffie came up with his Car. An early attempt at jet propulsion, it proposed a highly stream-lined, pear-shaped vehicle with a slight dent or curve in the roof, driven by a powerful jet of air which would go sweeping up over that dent to create a vacuum. Down the air would press to fill the vacuum and project the Car forward, presumably in a series of jerks. This caused endless trouble, particularly since none of us had a clue about vacuums! Griffie would end up in despairing rage, clamouring on about . . . 'a kind of piston arrangement!' . . . as fists flew and young bodies went hurtling all over the room.

We'd all submit our efforts to a communal verdict. Which was invariably harsh and frequently led to blows. At times, there'd be mayhem and we'd be expelled forthwith into the street. But we carried grimly on, determined to create *Our Own Magazine*, dedicated to Science, Science-Fiction and the Celebration of Youth. I was the one who used to keep the untidy, disordered mass of manuscripts with their scrawled corrections, incomprehensible diagrams and sweeping, undigested visions. At the time I thought they would one day burst on an Amazed, not to say Astounded world.

So we staggered on in our half-baked, terribly secretive style until that memorable day when a new magazine, *Modern Wonder*, suddenly appeared in Luvvie's. It caused almost as much of a sensation as

Picture Post did, about the same time—to be promptly bought on subscription by my father, to my insensate joy! *Lilliput* and *Men Only* produced joys of a different, unmentionable kind, pursued only at night, under the street lamp by Joe's the Fish Shop at the top of the street.

Modern Wonder transformed our situation. It was a boys' magazine devoted, of course, to Science, Science-fiction and the Celebration of Youth. I observed an article in it of mind-bending scientific precision so, shallowly cunning as ever, I left it ostentatiously around, in the hope of trailing *Amazing and Astounding* in its wake. My father, a teacher of physics and maths, was duly impressed and the Gang, transformed, emerged joyously from the Underground.

We used to spend hours in the kitchen, constantly arguing with copious reference to the magazine; endlessly, painfully rewriting our journal which marched on to no obvious destination; Griffie's Car a major source of disputation. Mam would bring us cups of tea now and then and occasionally demand silence for her endless, hypnotic quizzes.

Modern Wonder, however, had one side-effect. It was running a series on Youth Movements of the World and we were hypnotised by the Hitler Youth. We knew nothing of their ideas and cared less. All of us somehow in our guts knew that some day we'd have to fight these buggers; tribal osmosis, no doubt. But in the meantime, we were swept away by those gorgeous uniforms, the titles, the membership cards, the armbands!

In total dedication, we used to end all our meetings with the Hitler salute. We pinched their sonorous titles—terms like Ubersturmbannfuhrer and Reichsarbeitskommando were ever on our lips. There weren't enough of us to fill the posts so we had to double up on some positions—which couldn't have done much for the Fuhrerprinzip! I used to spend hours concocting hugely elaborate membership forms, very ornate, and we'd administer great oaths to the Fatherland and the Cause. We didn't know any of their songs, otherwise we'd have sung them. The one thing we lacked was armbands. But, with these trifling modifications, the Gwernllwyn

Chapel Gang started to act as a strictly extra-mural branch of the Hitler Youth.

It was at that point that an English Hot Gospeller came down and pitched his Tent on the great open space where later the Dowlais Recreation Ground was opened by Jennie Lee. (My father came back from that ceremony so starry-eyed that my mother threatened divorce, citing the Labour Party as co-respondent.) It was a great sweep of black dust, left by the old steel-works, with two big piles of stones, the Forts Niagara and Ticonderoga of our Saturday afternoon wars.

We were coming back from the Bryniau (which we pronounced Brinner) where we'd been playing cricket. We were all cluttered with bats and wickets as we made our way down, hopping along the old, disused rail-track. Davy Blackwell suddenly tackled Davy William and sent him sprawling while I was yelling 'Cut it out, you rodney!' and hurling a bat at his exposed legs, when The Man appeared.

He approached us, carrying something in his hand. Behind him, we could see the Tent billowing up and a big sign stretched right across it—Wales for Christ Crusade!—only one end wouldn't keep up. I can see him now. He was extraordinarily tall, his face the colour of Dowlas Furnace No. 2. He had a large adam's apple which kept wobbling up and down. He advanced on us, stretching out his hand.

'Men!' he called.

Men! We were transfixed.

He said, 'I need you! We must have a Captain for every Street!' And he held out his hand. It carried armbands.

Armbands!

We enrolled forthwith. We walked every street in our armbands, pushing leaflets calling on all to Come to Jesus through letter-boxes, accosting strangers in the street with News of the Cause. At the end of it we'd meet and salute each other with Fascist arms upraised. We tramped the streets of Dowlais, Storm Troopers for Christ.

And the Tent on Sunday was a revelation: the service was in English to start with! Religion in English was, to us, almost as much of a blasphemy as a joke in Welsh! The tent was packed with young kids from everywhere, kids we'd never seen before, kids singing their heads off. And the hymns! Welsh hymns. as you know, tend to the soulful, the mournful, occasionally the joyous and the always dramatic—*O Iesu mawr, rho d'anian bur*—and so on. Splendid, no doubt, but a little heavy on a dissident youth culture. But these hymns were jingles! We'd all sway and rock and clap hands to their beat.

I will make you Fishers of Men,
Fishers of Men, Fishers of Men,
I will make you Fishers of Men,
If you will follow me . . .

If you will follow me . . . in rising cadence—*ac felly yn ymlaen*! (and so on, to quote Chapel vernacular).

And there were Irish kids there, from the Bottom of Town, whom we'd never normally meet. There was one in particular. She was moving around putting out hymn sheets like a kind of prefect. She had a lithe body and green eyes. I went up to her, all elaborately casual like . . .

'Hello,' I said.

She looked up briefly and went on with her job. I picked up a few hymn-sheets and started putting them out on the seats.

'What's your name?' I asked.

'Hennessy,' she said.

Hennessy! God! I was stopped in my tracks. Memories of Corpus Christi processions came flooding back. Were Catholics Christian? Sundry horrific and totally inaccurate descriptions of Purgatory floated unbidden into my brain. Firmly suppressing them, I persisted . . .

'What's your first name?' I said.

She gave me one green eye over her shoulder. 'First names is for friends.'

I reeled back, took a deep breath, and carried on regardless . . .

'My name . . .' I began.

'I know your name,' she said. 'You're Froggy the teacher's son.'

I stood aghast. Dad! Froggy?

She went on remorselessly. 'I see you often,' she said, 'in Dowlais school. Through the railings . . .'

I felt rage surging up. 'Oh, aye?' I said. 'Free, was it?'

And she kicked me in the balls.

But on it went, Sunday afternoons and often during the week, Fishers of Men drowning out all competition. Disaster was inevitable. One Sunday night, our usual seat in the chapel gallery was deserted; we were up in the Tent, roaring and swaying away. The trouble is, it was the night of the *Cyrddau Mawr* (Big Meetings).

The Congregational Big Meetings were a regular affair. In Gwernllwyn, I was a minor star. I used to stand in the pulpit declaiming a suitably ethical poem in Welsh written by Brinley, the playwright rival to my uncle, mobilising all my carefully learned and conventional representations of emotion (which is still all the rage, I note, in Welsh Schools and their eisteddfodau, particularly in that practice which I consider a crime against humanity—the *cydadrodd* or communal recitation with its stylised, absolute and unchanging forms!) If I proved good enough, I'd be promoted to the great evening session in Bethania, the major chapel of the Independents in Dowlais, where I'd stand way up above the organ and pipe away at an audience which filled the chapel, in poems which invariably seemed to end in a suitably emotional . . . *'nes cyrraedd gwynfa lan* . . . until I reached the Heavenly Shore!'

But this Sunday, our entire gallery seat was empty. The consequences are best summed up by a phrase much used at the time—Ructions. In half a dozen little houses, beside the neatly laid tables and the endless wireless sets preaching war or the threat of war, we were all brutally introduced to the concept of Tribal Betrayal. The lesson got home. One night, we all sneaked up and threw stones at the Tent.

In that waste of black dust, as were huddling there throwing stones, pointlessly urged to get closer by a surprisingly manic Davy William, with a detached commentary from a cynical Glyn, we at last registered on the Tent, all lit up with kids' voices singing 'Fishers of Men'. Lights went up, men surged all around us, we fled panicking through a nightmare of dust, odd stones and holes. I gashed my knee and lay there in agony as they closed in. 'Sorry!' I said weakly, as I was haled into the Tent and prayed for in public . . . 'O Lord, forgive this Sinner!' . . . as I stood there writhing in the pillory, with scores of hostile young faces staring. I remember the utter contempt of Irish Green-Eyes to this day.

It is a horrible experience to be prayed for in public. It happened to me again many years later, when the universities fell to the first phase of Student Revolt, led at the time, improbable though it now seems, by Christian Fundamentalists, the Inter Varsity Federation. The IVF specialised in all the techniques which were later acquired wholesale by the Left—confrontation, occupation, demonstration. I was honking away in the big West Classroom in Aberystwyth, on some crucial topic like medieval Welsh land law, when a striking girl suddenly stood up and shouted 'God in Heaven! Have pity on this Sinner!'—a cry taken up at intervals by strategically placed colleagues about the room. I was reduced to utter speechlessness (a most unusual condition for a Dowlais man). It was worse for my boss, the Sir John Williams Professor; he was prayed for in public twice! He immediately married a PT instructress; I like to think he died happy.

This shattering experience of 'sinning', getting caught and then being humiliated in this way, was no less shattering for my father, who came to collect me. It was the first time I'd seen my father as a man. After that, I was plagued by it; wondered what made him tick. So one evening when they were out at the pictures, a regular ritual, I sneaked into what he called his study and the rest of us called the middle room. It was a tiny affair, packed with book shelves. My eye moved along his Masonic gear, the serried ranks of the *Tyst*, the Welsh Congregational journal, Labour Party minute books. Then it fell on a shelf of red and yellow covers—the Left Book Club. I took one down.

Today, I like to think it was Arthur Koestler's *Spanish Testament*, but it may not have been. I only know that it was about Spain. I was rooted to the spot for hours. The saga of the Spanish people and the horror and heroism of their Civil War gripped me by the throat. The International Brigade emerged as crusading knights, all the more so, since so many of them were Welsh! One piece still sticks in my mind.

I've learned since that Koestler admitted that a lot of the book was Comintern propaganda, but this story, I think, was true. A little peasant who was illiterate had joined the Republican army in order to learn to read. He was a prisoner in the same jail as Koestler, waiting to be shot, as usual on one of their filthy saints' days. The picture Koestler painted of him was savage and unforgettable—he ought to have been shipped to The League of Nations at Geneva in a cage labelled Ecce Homo 1937!

Later, as my father was busy with his pipe and paper, I tried my luck . . . 'Dad,' I said, 'what does Ecce Homo mean?' (My Form Three Latin hadn't progressed that far). There was a long pause. Then my father looked up and said, 'You've been at my books.' Another pause. Then he returned to his paper. 'All right,' he said, 'so long as you put them back.'

That was it. I devoured all those books, followed up by total immersion of a Baptist intensity in Dowlais Library with its books and newspaper section and even, twice, daring raids into Alien Territory in Merthyr Library! I took all the gang with me. Our heads were forever buried in books and journals. All around us Dowlais was wrestling with the Depression and the long, hopeless queues of the unemployed. We, locked into a kind of dream, hardly saw them.

We burned and bled with our comrades in Spain, with our people in the shelled Vienna flats. We became experts on the horrors of darkest Hungary, the agonies of Jugoslavia, the stifled hopes of Czechoslovakia. We relived the struggles—and the controversies—of the German Socialists and Communists, worshipped Rosa Luxemburg; we cheered on Leon Blum and the Popular Front in France—and everywhere. We even started on the Chinese and their Long March.

Gwernllwyn Chapel Gang became, almost overnight, an extra-mural branch of the Third International. In my case, the conversion was permanent.

We'd spend hours of an evening in a detached schoolroom which Gwernllwyn Chapel ran over the Bont. There, under the painting of *Jesus The Lamp of The World*, we wrestled with the various cretins' guides to Marxism then common. The Dialectic, I remember, caused us a lot of trouble. Griffie proved peculiarly obdurate, ignoring Davy William's painstaking elaboration of the reconciliation of opposites which he presented as if he understood it. He scorned my mocking cry of 'Griff, it's a kind of piston arrangement!'

Arguments raged even around our cricket matches on the Brinner. Not during them, of course; everything stopped for the leg break. We were engaged in a heated debate once, with much hurling of stumps, when a harsh, demanding voice cut in—'Where's your discipline, you silly buggers?' It was Moses, a little, seamed man we thought very old, with a probing, merciless line in political interrogation.

He must, I think, have been some kind of ancient dissident Communist. He took us up to his place, which was a fearful sort of hut right up on the Twynau, on the moors beyond Dowlais. We rarely ventured there and only in a gang because we were afraid of him. He'd rummage around in that smelly shambles and throw out crumbling, yellow journals for us to catch. I was not to see their like again until years later, when I was working on the early years of the International. 'Discipline! Discipline!' he'd snarl. 'You lot will never be Soldiers of the International.'

That's what caught us—the idea that we could be Soldiers of an International Army of many peoples, all working to the same end. We even got a hint of Communists as Jesuits! Oddly enough, the Soviet Union did not loom large. We knew something of the October Revolution, which confusingly for us was celebrated in November, but anything later didn't register at all; the dread name of Trotsky never crossed our lips. Russia was always there, of course, the Workers' Republic and as we all moved through the Munich crisis into the War, it loomed larger. In the War I bought a big *Daily Telegraph* war map on which Soviet Russia dominated continents in a bilious shade of yellow (well, it *was* the *Telegraph!*). In the depths of 1941 depression, I used to find consolation in its sheer size.

But for us, 13-14 year olds with all our familiar other interests, the intellectual training was minimal, to say the least. Russia was a far-off place of strange photographs of even stranger leaders. Though, naturally, the Hope of the World!

It was the idea of an International which gripped all of us by the throat. The Spanish Civil War, then in its last stages, was very big. South Wales provided volunteers, homes for the children from the Basque republic; there were rallies and collections innumerable. It was then that Iorri began to cast his shadow.

Iorri's father, a dedicated Communist activist, had gone to Spain, served briefly but came home to die of disease. With Iorri, we went to his burial. He had no religion, so they naturally gave him a Church of England funeral. There were crowds there, including Dowlais Spaniards. You could tell they were Spaniards. They wore brown boots and red ties and never spoke to the curate. And they gave him a Communist funeral, red flags and all. We all sang the *Internationale*.

Enthused, I rushed down to the International Brigade office near the remains of the old works, my head full of a 'Give me a gun and send me to Spain!' zeal. But as I shot in through the door, I froze. I stood there speechless. There was a high counter and, after a while, a face appeared over it. 'Oh!' it said, 'Young Williams, is it?' Our family were known in Dowlais as the Bloody Williamses. After another pause, he said . . . 'Son, come back when we're desperate.'

But we went on and on for months and years. We never joined anything or shared our feelings with anyone. We carried on, amid the myriad other things that occupied us, with our own private, secret Crusade. We thought everybody like us was doing the same. We were very surprised to find out, much later, that they weren't. Trying to be Soldiers of the International, we must have caught something of its spirit because we survived even the numbing horror of the Nazi-Soviet Pact.

In the end, though, we were beginning to split up under the decisive hammer of Matriculation, today's GCSEs, which splintered us and sent us on our separate ways. We came together for one last time on that Glorious Day, 22 June, 1941.

That morning, my father broke with precedent and came into

my bedroom with a cup of tea. 'You'll be all right now,' he said, 'they've gone into Russia.' I rushed through breakfast, snatching reports from the wireless, and dashed off to Gwernllwyn. The old gang was there, hopping about and hugging themselves. Whatever happened now, we knew we had won. And as people filed past into morning service, we sang the Internationale. *Sotto voce*, of course.

They're all gone now. Griffie James died years ago, after a short and wasted life. Davy Blackwell killed himself somewhere in England. Glyn vanished into Canada. I don't know what happened to Davy William. Gwernllwyn Chapel itself is long gone, They are ghosts of our Dowlais, which died years ago too. I am a ghost myself now, wandering about, digging them up out of their graves.

But there is one moment from those happy and silly years that still brings back powerfully the Gwernllwyn Chapel Gang which was my youth.

We heard that the Fascists, crawling out of their God-forsaken holes somewhere around Cardiff and Penarth, were coming up to stage a meeting in Dowlais. Our turf! They were going to hold it in Dowlais Top, by the Antelope pub and railway station. The very station where the trains from the Bedlinog pits used to bring miners home from work, including my grandfather. As a young child I used to stare at a sea of black faces until one of them singled me out and carried me to my grandmother. And the Fascists were going to meet there! And, moreover, they were going to hold their poisonous rally on a Sunday!

We were monumentally affronted and decided to join the counter-demonstration. Unfortunately, we had an important Sunday School to get through first. It turned out to be interesting. Our teacher was one of the younger, radical kind. After we'd read, impeccably, the parable of the loaves and fishes in Welsh and English, he leaned forward, with a glance over his shoulders towards his elders, all droning away at their prisoners. He said 'Know what I think? . . . I think He blackmailed the buggers into bringing out all the food they'd smuggled in with them!'

We were entranced; he sounded like one of the noble and brilliant authors we'd been mugging up on in the Bond schoolroom! We were so engrossed in this possible Marxist interpretation that we almost forgot the Great Demonstration of the Popular Front Against Fascism. But not quite.

Down to the cellars to unearth our banner—They Shall Not Pass! We'd argued for hours over the spelling of the Spanish version—one s or two? Iorri, consumed with impatience said, 'If we don't get a move on, the bloody Fascists will have gone!' So off we ran, up past the Dowlais Stables, and right up to Dowlais Top, trailing our misspelt banner—No Passaran! (We remembered the upside down exclamation mark at the beginning.)

We arrived just as the Fascists were in headlong retreat under a sea of missiles. Their armoured truck was trundling off, men in black pullovers scrambling on it. Our local communist-turned-fascist Arthur Eyles was still yelling away from the back. There was a brief glimpse of Moses, his face a picture of malevolent joy, hurling his egg. It exploded—kerplow!—right on Arthur's Fascist tie. Down they went to the bottom of Doctor's Pitch to a chorus of cheers, with a couple of black pullovers scuttling off into the ruins of the old works.

We were jumping up and down in ecstasy, Griffie yelling over and over, 'We beat them! We beat them!' when Iorri abruptly called us to order and told us to form up. So we marched, shouting at intervals. We marched through Dowlais, with little knots of Sunday afternoon strollers staring in mute disapproval. We marched down past the Guest School and the Guest Library, we marched on past the Guest Stables and the Guest Church on towards Station Road, past what was left of a Guest Steelworks, a road ready-made for a Triumph.

At that point, Iorri started to sing The Red Air Force Song:

> Our engines' roar the frozen air is cleaving
> Red Square is darkened by our guardian shade
> And over lands and polar oceans speeding
> Our cable lines of peace are laid.

Though we'd have had our tongues cut out rather than admit it, our hearts sank. We found these words very strange. Peace? Peace!

What had Peace to do with us? We wanted to bomb the bloody Fascists to hell and back!

But our hearts and voices rose into the hypnotic chorus . . .

> Fly higher! and higher! and higher!
> Our emblem the Soviet Star
> And every propeller was roaring . . .

A brief pause, and with fists clenched in salute, we roared at the shuttered wreck of the old Steelworks—RED FRONT!

> Defending the U.S.S.R.!

Over and over we sang that chorus as we marched along. Retribution was waiting, we knew, in those little houses with their neatly laid tables and their wireless sets preaching war and the threat of war. Retribution awaited all of us. But we didn't care!

We sang as we would never sing again and we marched as we would never march again, through a Dowlais which would never be again. And in our mouths was the taste of Victory!

Which was an unfashionable flavour that summer.

WELSH AND A SOCIAL DISEASE

'I could stay mum,' Griffie said. 'You know more than I do. You know
—you talk, I'll smile . . .'

'Griffie,' I said, 'watch it!'

'But I couldn't even say good morning!' Griffie said.

'Of course you can,' said I. 'Look, all we have to do is get
through the official thing, make do with the usual Hello and Thank
You—and then get lost in the herd.'

The man in the seat opposite suddenly leaned forward and
spoke. 'Boys, the aim of the Camp isn't to stop you talking English,'
he said, 'it's to encourage you to speak Welsh.'

He was one of the *swyddogion*, the officials of the Urdd! We stared
at him petrified, as the train wound its interminable way from
Carmarthen towards Aberystwyth, the guard hopping out now and
again to pick flowers.

Griffie and I were off on our last adventure together—a week at
the Urdd Camp at Llangrannog. The Urdd—*Urdd Gobaith Cymru*
(the League of the Hope of Wales, literally) was the Welsh-speaking
Youth Movement, full of the Greek ideals of a Healthy Mind in a
Healthy Body which were common at the time even in the
Woodcraft Folk, the Communist answer to the Scouts. Though
there were dark rumours in the Valleys that the Urdd's founder had
been influenced by Fascism.

It was not the dominant influence in Welsh-speaking Wales it has
since become, but it was quite powerful, with language classes, eisteddfodau, cruises and so on. My aunt used to go on the cruises—
strictly 'Celtic' you understand—to Cornwall, Brittany and Galicia.

There were four recognised pillars of Welshness among us—the
Chapel, the Eisteddfod, Aberystwyth University College and the
Urdd, all of them Irredeemably Respectable. My father had never
shown much interest, but in 1939, in one of his periodical fits of
Welshness, he decided I must go to the famous Urdd summer camp
at Llangrannog 'to do me good'.

I learned later that it was a very distinguished camp. Siân Phillips the actress was there; so were a famous architect, and an equally famous BBC man. It was the Welsh equivalent of a Good Public School!

But at the time, I was in a panic. I begged for company—and Griffie was dragooned in as my companion, presumably at the prompting of his mother, ever yearning for respectability. Because if the Urdd was anything it was certainly Respectable.

Today, among a small people riven by an unutterably stupid chasm over language which threatens to expel us from history, it is difficult to recall how I actually felt at the time. We felt superior to the generality certainly and with reason. Valleys culture was international and rich. But we in no sense felt that Welsh was inferior. If anything it enjoyed some sense of moral worth—Eminently Respectable, for sure. Certainly, having spoken English only since I was six, I felt guilt over not being fluent in Welsh. But Good Lord, I spoke it well enough, read it, was taking it as a secondary school subject, had even broadcast on BBC Wales in it! I can't understand why I was so scared at the prospect of the Urdd camp. But scared I was—and Griffie, who never heard any Welsh outside chapel, was worse.

My mother tended to denigrate her own Welsh—which was totally unnecessary, though common enough throughout Wales. 'Carmarthen Welsh is the purest form of Welsh,' Mam used to pronounce (of course, her father came from Cil-y-Cwm), 'though North Walians, of course, speak Oxford Welsh.' I used to stare fixedly at my grandmother who was a Gog, as North Walians came to be known. Oxford? At the very least, it would have to be Oxforrrrd!

So scared witless we were, the two of us, as we headed into west Wales. In the event, it worked out. West Walians and even Northerners seemed quite human. People were much more tolerant, then, than they have apparently since become. But the first few days were an ordeal.

We had to take part in the evening *noson lawen*—a kind of self-entertainment. Fortunately, I'd mastered a somewhat sardonic Welsh song about an old harpist in the vale of Llangollen who'd starved to death; to his funeral came enough food to keep him alive.

26

Funerals were in truth a major feast. 'Did you have a good funeral?' they used to ask. 'Tongue,' came the measured reply. 'Tongue!' Tongue was certainly *de rigueur* at such communal festivals—my parents considered it an Absolute Necessity, when in Aberystwyth much later, we were paid a State Visit by the Mayor of Merthyr. Tongue seems to have been as much of a cherished delicacy as hot peppered chops were to the Middle Ages, to judge from the *Mabinogion*.

Anyway, with the Vale of Llangollen—and Griffie providing a tum-tum-tum accompaniment—the *noson lawen* rite of passage we survived, and soon got lost in the camp routine, even if it were conducted in what was, in essence, a foreign language.

The boys were in tents at one end of the field, the girls in huts at the other and there were huts for various purposes scattered around. In them, we went through a resolutely minded drill of sports, exercises, endless language practice and of course Cultural Experiences. It was the sing-songs which stood out.

Those songs were great. They nearly all went to the tune of 'She'll Be Coming Round the Mountain When She Comes' (shades of 'Fishers of Men'!)—and they pre-empted the student songs of Aberystwyth much later.

There was one in wordplay on various fruits and vegetables—

Banana, BanaNANa, BANaNA!

and so on, through potato, tomato and the rest, with cucumber sung with peculiar emphasis—

Cucumber, CucumBUMber, CucumBER.

There was another about Johnnie Morgan's Whiskers which he swore never to shave until he got his BA.!

'*B.A. neu'r Bedd!*' was the cry—B.A. or the Grave. And Mr Morgan seems to have taken almost a lifetime to achieve his degree.

'WHISKIT! Whiskit, 'co Whiskers Johnnie Morrgan!'

Repeat *ad infinitum*. Till the chorus—

"Co Whiskers Johnnie Morrgan ar y llawr
Mynd lan i gael B.A.!'

We chorused lustily, as he went up to get his cherished B.A., with his whiskers sweeping the floor!

We were regaled with contemporary songs about ourselves (the 'topicals' of Aberystwyth) and the current situation. One classic went—

Mae Hitler yn mynd i Poland, meddan nhw! . . .
Hitler's going into Poland, so they say!

Greeted with a tremendous chorus of—

TWLL DIN I ADOLF HITLER!! meddan nhw!
ARSEHOLES TO ADOLF HITLER!! meddan nhw!

It echoed round the Camp constantly. If it were true that the Urdd had been founded with semi-Fascist ideas in mind, then something must have gone terribly wrong somewhere!

Then there were Sports. Swimming was a particular delight, around a great rock on the beach. And it was there I met Bethan from Blaenau Ffestiniog. She was inescapable, anyway. A vigorous young blonde who took a fancy to me, she'd rush at me, bear me to the ground and fumble about with strong, inquisitive fingers. I was at the age when, confronted with girls running at you, you took off smartish in the opposite direction!

I remember once being pushed by Bethan up a hill. At the top, as I lay exhausted, warding off her hands and revelling in her throaty laughter, I noticed the evening scenery of Cardigan Bay, which struck me as marvellous. I still find it so.

There were girdles of lights everywhere. A particularly brilliant one lay to the north. 'What's that?' I said. She replied, 'It's Aberystwyth.' It was actually, I now suspect, Aberaeron.

But if Bethan said it was Aber, Aber it was. And there she blew! Aberystwyth was a legend of my youth. The People's College, 'built on the pennies of the poor', as they said, the College which was the

28

theme of innumerable University Sundays in our Chapel. The college of my grandmother's inexorable 'Higherr and Aberr! . . . doctorr, preacherr or teacherr!'

'That's where I'm going,' I declared. I did, too.

The day raced on, in mingled fear and joy. But the nights were something else!

In the evening, the two older Dowlais boys in our tent (in that tent we always spoke English) would get out the illegal cards. They were Old Urdd Hands. They'd even smoke, equally illegally, as Griffie and I stared out at them, speechless with admiration, from our sleeping bags.

They used to be joined by a friend, an Even Older Urdd Hand. He was called Llanberis, presumably because he came from there. He had a positive gift for ruthless hypnosis, aided by a peculiarly manic eye. He'd hold us spellbound with all his terribly knowledgeable talk.

But one night, after some muttered confabulation with the other two, he decided it was Our Turn . . . God, that night!

Putting aside the cards and drawing heavily on his daring cigarette, he leaned forward to fix us with his glittering eye. He pronounced—

'This Camp is DANGEROUS!'

We sat up, stunned. There was a momentous pause.

'How do you mean?' I said.

He leered knowingly. Then he said, 'VD! That's what I mean. VD. It's a miracle half of us haven't gone down with it.'

Griffie and I, noses above the blanket, stared in petrified horror.

'VD!' went on Llanberis, thundering out the Unmentionable. 'You can catch it anywhere. ANYWHERE. Particularly here. In this Camp!'

'What are you talking about?' said I.

'All these boys and girls,' said Llanberis. 'All that physical contact.' He pronounced the words as if they were leprous, with a terrible shudder and a rolling of those eyes. Then a vague, sweeping gesture, 'You can get it ANYWHERE.'

There was a pregnant pause.

29

Llanberis fixed his malevolent eye on me. 'You know about VD?' he said.

I lay there, beginning to tremble.

I was accustomed to, shall I say, the mechanics of sexual intercourse. I had been introduced to them graphically by a boy in the lane behind my grandmother's house. I'd felt physical stirrings in sundry grapplings with girls in shop doorways. Not to mention Bethan. I had been peculiarly disturbed by a leaflet advertising the film *King Kong*, which had a girl spread-eagled across it, her skirt hitched up to her neck, her knickers prominently on show! Haunted my nights for weeks.

But the Awful Penalties we knew of, too. We knew that if you tossed yourself off—Count Toby Tostoff, a Ruined Pole, was a folk hero—you'd go blind. But VD was the nameless horror that, like a ferocious ghoul, stalked the night. We knew vaguely there were two forms—gonorrhea and syphilis, which sounded like daughters of King Lear. The first was less harmful—only your nose would drop off. But the second!—ugh! horror!—you'd end up a gibbering wreck or even turn into a Werewolf. So we knew about VD.

'Yes,' I squeaked at Llanberis.

'Aha!' said he, meaningfully silent. 'You've got to watch it.' Then, with a sweeping gesture that had VD carried on spores in the air— 'EVERYWHERE. Touching hands! Touching other parts! Laughing and running around . . . everywhere!'

There was another long pause as we digested this hair-rising information.

Llanberis turned his frightful eye on me.

'You,' he said, 'You! You've got to be particularly careful.'

'What?' said I.

'I've seen you,' he said, 'with that Bethan.'

I yelped— 'I was only splashing her!'

'AHA,' came the terrible cry, conjuring up swiftly suppressed memories of Bethan's unremitting physical presence, 'Aha! YOU CAN GET IT EVERYWHERE!'

Silence.

Then Llanberis leaned forward with his manic eye roaming around the tent. 'Lavatory seats!' he said, 'L-A-V-A-T-O-R-Y S-E-A-T-S.'

Lavatory seats! Good God, was nothing sacred? Not even in Welsh?

We stared out of hypnotised eyes above the blankets. Griffie in the end squawked— 'How can we know?'

'Ah,' said Llanberis. 'There IS a way!'

He fumbled around and brought out a penny. 'See this?'

We nodded dumbly.

'Well,' he said, 'If you press this against the end of your . . . you know, John Willy . . .', (a pause to let the full horror sink in), '. . . if it burns, you've got it. If it doesn't, you're clear.'

Another silence

'Aw, don't be daft,' I cried, wrapping the blanket around me furiously and turning to desperately willed sleep.

There was a burst of laughter from the older boys. Then Llanberis stubbed his fag out to leave. Opening the tent flap, he paused, outlined against the sky. 'Remember,' he said, his manic eye shining, 'L-A-V-A-T-O-R-Y S-E-A-T-S!' and he was gone.

I lay there for hours sleepless. In the end, I HAD TO KNOW. But I couldn't face the shame of barging out through the tent flap. After much fumbling about, I found a penny. Then I shuffled near the tent edge and started to work up some of the pegs.

It took ages, but ages, till, in the end I had two of them inched up, in deadly silence, enough to let me out. A painful wriggle through and I stood up in the night air.

I could see nothing. It was pitch black. With arms outstretched, I stumbled across the Field of the Camp of the League of Welsh Hope. At last I felt wood under my fingers and knew I was there.

I was bowled over by some-one rushing out. It was Griffie. As I sprawled there in shame, he yelled aloud, 'I haven't got it!' and dashed off into the dark.

I rushed in. I came out shaking. I had it! I had VD!

I crashed back into the tent, oblivious to everything and every-one and slumped there in the dark. I never slept all night. I was seized with the ultimate horror.

31

How was I going to tell Mam? Tell her that I had VD. And in the URDD CAMP AT LLANGRANNOG . . .

But in the morning, a Friday, Hitler did indeed go into Poland. It was Arseholes to Adolf Hitler—and I forgot all about my VD.

In later years, after the war, I went looking for Llanberis. He was dead. He'd been in Bomber Command and was lost over Germany.

You've got to watch out. It's EVERYWHERE.

WELCOME TO FRANCE

We pushed off at night. We crowded the deck as the craft nosed its way out, and threaded through long lines of ships between the subdued coast lights. We headed south from Newhaven into the Channel . . . Norway bound, no doubt.

Many years later, I convinced myself that we landed in Normandy on the evening of D-Day, 6 June. It couldn't have been that soon. But it couldn't have been much later. For as we crouched on the deck that night, we heard on the radio Wynford Vaughan Thomas, the celebrated war correspondent, hailing the liberation of an unscathed Rome on 5 June, the eve of D-Day.

Many years later, I was to be heavily involved with Wynford in a TV history of Wales, but in 1944, he was a familiar voice on the radio. On 5 June I listened to that voice locked into a kind of ecstacy over the preservation of the ancient monuments of Rome, and wondered uneasily what my father would think. He was one of the Bomb Rome Now brigade; if any ancient monuments disappeared in the process, well they were Fascist, weren't they? And if they weren't Fascist, they were bloody Catholic!

An American voice suddenly cut in . . . 'Say,' it said, 'who's this guy? Got the gift of the gab, hasn't he?' I could but agree . . . 'But his accent,' went on the sailor, 'kinda funny, no? . . . Is he English?' I pointed out a fundamental error . . . 'Welsh?' said the sailor . . . 'What's that?' I tried to explain . . . 'Is that so?' he said, eyeing with deepening suspicion the sawn-off runt of the species before his eyes . . . 'You know this guy?' . . . 'Of course,' I said, lying in my teeth, 'he's my cousin . . .'

The weather worsened, so below, in trepidation, as the waves got up, I lay there in my rolling, pitching bunk, sleepless, for what seemed an eternity. I was full of foreboding, as the sea heaved beneath us.

I must have looked like a Christmas tree. A great mountain of packs and equipment with two tiny duck's feet emerging. My boots were a size too big anyway. It was in a state of acute discomfort that

I finally lurched on deck on a chill morning to take my place in the queue as we closed in on the Normandy coast.

It was a little east of Arromanches but still on Gold Beach. We could hear the crump of guns inland with the great battleships offshore letting loose their deafening salvoes. My vision narrowed down to what I could see in front, underneath my tin hat. Vaguely aware of the sea around us, buzzing with landing craft, dead and alive, with the odd burning ship, we could see bits of Mulberry Harbour being towed into position. Offshore there was a great contraption with deep sea divers. The noise was all engulfing, with aircraft zooming overhead, ships weaving in and out of our path, men shouting. A kind of disciplined confusion gripped us all. What we had to do was get ashore and up that beach—a narrow strip with hundreds of men and vehicles, tanks and transporters burning, the odd zip of bullets and inexplicable explosions—up a narrow hill past a church with a great bite out of its roof, a French tricolour stuck into it, along a path over a hill. The whole world narrowed down to that strip, as the craft closed in on it, in a cacophony of noise.

The ramps grated at last on the first stanchions of Mulberry and we were down. I waddled on the ramp for as long as I could and then jumped in. The water, in an ice-cold shock, came right up to my waist. I let out an anguished shout but waddled on, my rifle held high over my head. I was aware of nothing but a terrible fatigue as I inched forward, every step an agony. It seemed ages before I could feel the dry land under my oversized boots, as men kept yelling at us.

Across that beach, with your feet dragging in the sand, until at last you were out, over the seawall with a glimpse of ordinary houses behind, right under that church with a bite taken neatly out of its Gothic roof and its tricolour limply defiant.

The first thing I saw was a British Army cross marking a grave with the name Handel Evans on it. I had a friend back home called Handel Evans, a big, empty man, very confident with a line of patter to match, who later tried to get off with my girl friend. But at that time, I thought he was dead. Brooding was a luxury we

34

couldn't afford. Harangued on all sides, we laboured up that bloody hill which never seemed to end, to reach the top at last and to rest.

I turned to look back—and was suddenly seized with a terrible exultation . . .

The scene opened up in a breath-taking panorama. The whole sea seemed full of ships; you could have walked back to Newhaven on the decks. Thousands of men were pouring ashore, milling around the beach, tanks leading them off. Over our heads was a continuous roar and the sky was dark with aircraft. The sheer impact of all that mass of men, material, aircraft and ships was overwhelming. I stood there astounded. It was one of my two historic moments.

And in strict partisan and private manner, I felt a vaulting exhilaration. These were our men, our ships; the air was black with our airplanes. All those years of defeat came flooding back. We'd been shelled in the Vienna flats and driven underground; we'd been defeated in Spain after a heroic struggle and driven out of history. And the catalogue of defeat rolled on . . . Czechoslovakia, Poland, France, the Balkans . . . But now, NOW it was WE who were victorious, we who were driving the Fascist bastards back, we who were going to tear down their ghastly edifice of lies and hypocrisy and murder, smash their army and their lousy camps and march right across Europe to link hands with the heroic Red Army!

It was like that dream of the balcony of Merthyr Town Hall and the Revolution but this time, I could see it happening. Or at least, I thought I could.

And it was with renewed commitment that I clomped down the hill and hitched my Christmas tree of a carcase along the path inland. It took hours and hours. Long before the end of it, my exhilaration had vanished. I remember nothing but awkwardly plodding in my boots, in which my ankles turned, past field after field, sometimes with a dead cow in them, its four legs sticking straight up in the air. I caught the first whiff of the smell which, thereafter, would sum up Normandy in 1944 to me—the sickly, sour smell of dead horses. We finally came into the village of Ryes near Bayeux. There, a Reinforcement Holding Unit was supposed to be awaiting our Regiment of Odds and Sods. It had yet to land!

There was nothing for it but to dig slit trenches to sleep in, what were later called foxholes a l'Americain. It was murder. The ground was like hardened concrete and it took hours. It came to rain and we stretched tarpaulins across and lay under them, spent.

After a while the rain stopped and I drifted out into the field. You could hear the guns in the distance but otherwise it was silent. I wondered uneasily whether Out There, there was anything between us and the Germans. There must have been —and with a shrug I wandered off down a hill to where a disused railway line ran. There was a dim lantern not far away and I thought I could see something on the rail. It turned out to be Penydarren Iron Co!

My home town. I drifted back across that moonlit field desperately homesick. I decided to pack it in. I clambered down into my ill-dug pit, put my hand on the rifle to make sure and tried to sleep.

Sometime in the night, I heard a scrabbling just outside the trench. Panicking, I brought my rifle up, cocked it and stared into a blackness with some faint whispers of moonlight . . . 'Psst. Hey, Tommy!' came a hoarse, rusty voice. I stared up and could just make out a face with bristles looming over the edge . . . 'Tommy! Psst!' it said . . . 'Calvados? Calvados, eh?' waving an un-labelled bottle.

I stared back. I didn't know what a Calvados was! I hardly drank at all then. I stirred and before I knew what was happening a wiry, little figure clambered into the trench and squeezed up beside me. His leprechaun's face leered. He was like a sprightly little monkey with a face all bristles.

He opened the bottle and passed it over. Enormously relieved, I swigged at it . . . God, if the Germans had attacked the next morning, one sector of the British front could have offered no resistance at all.

Then, up he shinned out of the trench. And with a careless wave of the hand, he called in his thick Norman French . . . 'Tommy! Welcome to France!'

THE SERGEANT AND THE GENERAL

There followed months of unremitting boredom. The Reinforcement Holding Unit, when it landed, housed us in tents, but what were they to do with us? None of us was from a particular unit; some like me needed hundreds of miles between us and the enemy to fulfil our allotted trades! I had a brief spell in Beach Signals, but otherwise, like the rest, I was condemned to a nightmare of spud-bashing and endless lying around.

I remember a few moments—the solitary soldier who made it his duty to milk a few Norman cows to ensure their survival; the crowd that came in from units which had disgraced themselves in combat and lived in a mood of intense gloom. In contrast, there was a squad of very young Guardsmen who passed through once. Harassed by their high-pitched words of command which came out in every case as — 'Company! Hipe!'—I was astonished when, after being harangued on their imminent departure for The Front, they all rushed off, mad and roaring with excitement, desperately eager to Get At It. I often wonder what happened to all of them.

Otherwise, it was the truck to Bayeux, much run down at the time, a pointless evening in cafes and a mass pissing against the Cathedral as we waited for the truck back.

In later years, Normandy became a favourite of mine. I found the region marvellous, the people warm and friendly. No doubt the experience was haunted by memory. In a restaurant once, having sampled the multi-lingual joys of the Tapestry in a gleaming, glittering gem of a Bayeux, I caught a glimpse through the window of a Highland Division sign, put up as a directional guide and since polished and maintained as a memorial to those far-off days of 1944; I remembered the original. But most of us in 1944 found Normans at best taciturn, at worst grim.

It is hard to blame them. They'd had enormous Allied armies decanted into their strip of land; their towns and cities had been bombed and shelled to ruins. It was a wonder they survived at all.

Their plight first struck me in Ryes as a gang of us were making our way back to base. Some poor devil of a farmer was pleading with the local wineshop to open for him, but the patron refused, 'because of the soldiery'. I appreciated their situation acutely at that moment. What would Glamorgan have been like with half a million troops decanted into it? As it was, it was bad enough! But for most of us, the breakout into a welcoming France came as a huge relief.

I was more fortunate than most. Almost on my first visit to Bayeux, I ran into the Leprechaun with the Calvados. (I've had a taste for it ever since!) He hailed me as a long-lost son and introduced me to his kin who ran a little cafe just off one of the main squares, today named after General de Gaulle. I spent those months esconced in that Norman family. They were the patrons, a young girl, an even younger boy and a very sophisticated cousin evacuated from Paris who seemed to have been a prostitute, although clearly a high-class one. We used to have long philosophical conversations.

My stilted sixth-form French developed very swiftly. I used thoroughly to enjoy the long talks with the patron and his friends, though I was inordinately harassed by the many British mates I immediately acquired, all bent on cultivating *la Parisienne*! It was 'you talk, I'll smile,' all over again.

I was even more embarrassed by the young girl, 14 years old who developed a fearful crush on me. I remember acutely embarrassing moments in shop doorways, when her passion got the better of her —moments not improved by my mates who offered unwanted advice on how to cope with her 'undeveloped' sexual organs. I used to feel hot with shame to find her father's reproachful eye on her when we returned to the cafe. Like most Frenchmen, he'd been in the army —and it was the women they blamed! God, I even stopped pissing on their Cathedral as a gesture.

But really, I had a good time with them. I even spent my nine-teenth birthday in the cafe, when they opened for me a bottle of champagne they'd been saving for the Peace.

In many visits to an absolutely polished and Euro-chic Bayeux in later years, I used to dodge that cafe—though I remember bursting into tears in my hotel room on the night of my first return. But in the end, I went back there.

It was still largely a working-class place, untouched by all the glamour around. I sat there with my Calvados and suddenly started talking to the few customers, telling them of the birthday I spent in that very place. They were what passes in Normandy for enthusiastic and after I bought one drink, the patron refused my offer of payment—unheard-of for a Norman. I think he was the very young boy of 1944.

It could not last. Officers came around the Reinforcement Holding Unit one day, commandeering our Army records. I found I'd been classed as a Marksman and was issued with a Bren gun. I became a member of a motley crew mobilised into an Infantry Support Group attached, however loosely, to the 43rd Wessex Division, then moving into a slaughterhouse engagement on Hill 112. Hill 112 commanded a view over the *bocage* and Caen and was much disputed. We went into rapid training and it was there that I had the encounter with The Sergeant.

The Sergeant was much older, a craggy, tough, unsentimental but generous man who radiated Experience and the Confidence it brought. I was a much-mothered youth from south Wales, my head stuffed full of dogmatic illusions. Yet we became very close, in a strictly heterosexual but intense relationship. He took me over like a gruff but kindly step-father—cook's tea, the extra blanket, an encouraging snarl, a reassuring curse at a critical moment.

He had fought with the International Brigade in Spain and used to regale us with yarns about barracks life in Albacete, the enthusiasm and ignorance of the militias, the fighting of Jarama, the farewell parade in Barcelona. The Civil War in Spain was to me absolutely formative: I hero-worshipped him.

Then, as we neared Hill 112, over the fire and the cook's tea one night, he passed around some hideous photographs and casually revealed that he had also been one of the Black and Tans in Ireland after the First World War.

Today, I suppose, perched on the cool pinnacles of our historical and sociological imagination, we might find such conduct explicable.

The Sergeant was no mercenary or war-lover, though he cherished soldiering. Hostility to Catholicism, I suspect, may have been a motive. In his time the Spanish and Irish Catholic Churches must have seemed black holes in the humanity of Europe.

But in Normandy in 1944, I was eighteen, I was Welsh, I was a member of a Welsh Independent Chapel and of the Young Communist League. I saw everything in Black and Red. With a man who had been a member of both the Black and Tans and the International Brigade, I simply could not cope. To paraphrase Winston Churchill, up with that I would not put.

I withdrew my ambassadors. The Sergeant was monstrously and visibly offended. He put me in mind of a *tyrannosaurus rex* in a temper.

We came to Hill 112, or some rise near it, and walked up it. The Germans had everything ranged and down came the mortars. We ran off it. Unfortunately, I ran off without my Bren gun. The Sergeant thrust his face into mine and said, 'Right, hook your Taff arse back up that hill and pick up that Bren, you yellow little Welsh bastard.' It was an unwelcome experience, like climbing Cader Idris in a snowstorm.

From that moment, hatred of the Sergeant possessed me. It was a pure, burning, virginal sort of hatred, such as I was not to experience again until my first interviews on Welsh television. I determined to take the Sergeant's rancid English words and ram them down his English Black and Tan throat. I began to perform deeds of insouciant but visible valour—to no avail, since he got his English International Brigade head blown off shortly afterwards.

A memorable experience? I think so now. But at the time, in the press of events, I clean forgot the Sergeant. In my many visits to Normandy in later years, I tended half-deliberately to avoid Hill 112. Recently, however, the memory resurfaced and gripped me by the throat. I went back to Hill 112.

And I couldn't find it! In the end, I discovered it only because the 43rd Wessex Division had raised a memorial there.

Hill 112, in 1944 a monstrous, threatening height, from which I once saw the RAF bomb the daylights out of Caen—and a futile exercise that was—was, in 1985, amid the ruthlessly shaven *bocage*, a pale and gentle rise. What is the truth—Hill 112 as a pimple or as Cader Idris in a snowstorm?

No doubt, a proper, professional historian would recognise a truth in both experiences and, following the precepts of the craft, try to locate each in its historical context and to set both in historical perspective. This is difficult at the best of times. If you have actually been there yourself, twice, it is even harder.

Not that I had much time for such reflection. Our Support Group went through a kind of hell. Our first officer, I think from the Indian Army, did not last long. His idea of tactics was—'Five Panzer tanks in front! Fix bayonets! Charge!' He was removed in circumstances of near mutiny. But we lost three officers in almost as many days. I was rocketed up to Sergeant and to authority.

I think, in fact, that I missed my vocation. Tank-busting—because that became our function—developed into a passion. I remember hours passed poring over diagrams of German tanks under the lamplight, seeking their weak spots. I remember the joy with which I greeted our first 17-pounder gun which at last put us on an equal footing with the Fascist bastards. But it was a fearful strain—I was an eighteen-year-old who had to exercise authority, in all my five foot and a fart stature, over men many years my senior. It was hellish.

I remember one road in particular. Empty roads became an obsession. With all the din of battle rather distant, an empty road would register as 'silence'. Cigarette packets were the key. If the road was littered with the Anglo-American variety, well and good; if the litter was German, we knew what to do. But if they were French, what the hell could anyone think?

This one road had nothing, so we advanced slowly in proper style, spread out, down it. I, in front, was staring ahead as if my life depended on it, as I suppose it did. There was a moment—I remember it still—when looking down this quite short road to a T-junction, I thought I saw, through a corner glass window, into a hedge and behind it, like a child's tracery, the outline of a Tiger tank!

I called a couple of the older men up but they could see nothing. So we resumed our crawl down that road. Every so often I'd call a halt and we'd all dive to the ground. It was as hot as hell; I could feel the impatience and hostility grate on the back of my neck. But I carried on with the frog-like crawl. 'Taff, what the hell are we doing, stooging around like this?'— one of them broke discipline and yelled. I ignored it. But in the last resort, I couldn't stand it. I stood up and said, 'O.K., you sods! Let's walk.'

It was at that point that the bloody Tiger opened fire. It took us a day and a half to reduce it. It was like besieging Harlech Castle. So I was hugely relieved when we were pulled out and I could revert to being a Reinforcement Holding Unit waster again.

Back to Ryes and the old routine . . . but as the front began to break up, the Americans raced ahead, the French approached Paris and the British were grinding up to the Seine, the Unit was seized with activity.

Officers came around again, rooting out, this time, Signals personnel. I, of course, with an A-class trade, was one of the first targets. We were formed into a cloak-and-dagger unit which remains to me a mystery to this day. Our target was Paris!

Paris was in the American zone and had been earmarked for liberation by Leclerc's First French Division. There was a story that we were to install scramblers for that French division—this was so implausible no-one believed it. Among us there were dark hints of Phantom—an ultra hush-hush unit whose shadowy existence haunted us. Another bet was that we were to go on reconaissance to fix a site for the British section of SHAEF—Supreme Headquarters Allied Expeditionary Force. I have never heard anything anywhere about that mission. Maybe it was just cooked up by bored officers. I just didn't know and I don't know.

What I do know is that we careered off, two jeeps and a truck, cutting behind the advancing armies, going on all sorts of detours, like Ernest Hemingway's amateur group at the same time. It was a triumphant procession. In town and village, it was cheering crowds, bottles of wine and girls all the way. We were particularly popular in American zones, where British soldiers were rarely seen and Americans not much liked. I remember it all as a blur of cheers, laughing faces, girls' mouths and bottles of wine.

We came into northern Paris, where firing was still going on, right through to Montmartre, straight into the Place Pigalle. The Brass made the mistake of billeting us in a building just off the Place—Pig-alley, as it came to be known though not to me, who cherished visions of Tolouse-Lautrec and all that. The next morning as we mustered on parade in an inner square, we discovered that one whole wall of windows to one side belonged to a House full of Daughters of Joy, to quote the vernacular.

While we stood stiffly to attention below, the girls would crowd the windows, giggling and calling, going through various stages of strip-tease, as we remained expressionless. In the end, they started to inflate French letters into balloons and float them down. As they came floating past our rifles, I wished we had bayonets.

But that was it! Out we were hustled, to set up in tents in some Bois or other. And it was there that we were given the day off (from what I can't think) to see General de Gaulle make his ceremonial entry into Paris. It was my second historic moment.

Everywhere, great crowds of people were milling about, shouting, crying, singing. Young women in summer dresses rippled like sweeps of flowers into the gutters at the sound of gunfire. Through it all moved General de Gaulle, with a cigarette drooping from his mouth—just like Jean Gabin in those French films we used to sneak down to Cardiff to watch over and over through an afternoon and an evening.

We were outside Notre Dame as he moved in, with his arms stretched out in his usual awkward gesture. We were there when snipers opened up on him inside Notre Dame. Every one dived to the floor—except de Gaulle, who just stood there, tall and statuesque, singing, I presume a *Te Deum*, in his peculiar plonking voice. I remember being inordinately impressed as I joined everyone else to shuffle shamefaced to my feet. I'm less impressed now—if you're going to be Joan of Arc, you have to live the part.

Outside, there was pandemonium. They'd brought up tanks and started to shell Notre Dame! We all thought the snipers were French Fascists but they turned out to be members of the Japanese embassy staff, making a last stand in good old Okinawa style.

We were there when de Gaulle swept out past us into the square which was heaving. He stretched out his arms and said '*Mes camarades!*' It must have been the last time he said that. The square was full of FTP, the Francs Tireurs Partisans—the Communist Resistance. They all went mad. There was a tremendous roar and a forest of rifles went up outside the facade of Notre Dame.

I was swept by enthusiasm. I decided there and then to devote the rest of my life to the history of the French Revolution.

In the event, I was to graduate as an English medievalist.

SOLDIERS OF THE INTERNATIONAL

'*Ah, Taffy!*' Charmaine murmured in my ear, as she thrust her breast even more firmly into my dilated eye and wrapped her leg around my waist, '*tu m'as bouleverse ma vie de jeune fille!*'—or words to that effect.

Good-Oh! thought I, as I burrowed still further into her lovely neck, in our mutual writhing on the back seat of a French cinema, totally oblivious to what was, no doubt, another French classic on screen. I revelled in having overturned her life as a young girl. Charmaine the adorable, the unattainable, queen of our little world, with her breath on me, her legs around me, her skirt riding high under my hands!

Then wham! The lights suddenly went up and in total bewilderment I felt people heaving and leaving all around.

My French friends swooped, in a noisy mob, and half-carried me, still in transports of unconsummated passion, down the stairs, out into the street and up more stairs, into a room where a French band was blasting away, accordions in full cry—the local hop.

Dede, my mate, was there, solemn as usual, bestowing the favour of his saturnine presence on occasional females; Bernard, squat and stolid, would sometimes stir himself to take part, while Guy, suave and silky in his American jacket, wove in and out with grace and Latin American abandon.

I, still dazed, put in a few obligatory twirls with Bernard's sister, the puritanical Lisette, who moved her body around with care and precision like a holy chalice . . . and Charmaine, ah Charmaine!—would swirl around us, hypnotising young males innumerable, no doubt overturning their whole lives as young men . . . while I lowered there like a spavined buffalo, till the clock struck and I thought 'Christ Almighty! The Truck!'

Out then, with a shout— '*Faut partir!*'—to cheers from the crowd of them, down the stairs, and out to the corner where the Red Ball Express, an American priority highway drove its way right past the

45

houses where Bernard's home was; an unremitting thunder, as one enormous and inhuman truck followed another, racing by with supplies for the Front, ruthlessly overriding all opposition. They sent child after child into hospital, the mothers' agonised cries ignored.

A mad dash across that desperate road into the deep, deep peace of the unit truck and its anonymous darkness. We slewed up through the night, my brain still reeling, into our barracks on the hill.

It was Versailles, where I spent nine blissful months in Supreme Headquarters Allied Expeditionary Force, SHAEF for short, as a sergeant, a strictly courtesy title because of my Trade—to quote the Signals vernacular: unpaid, unwashed, unwept, unhonoured and unsung.

Getting there though had been a bit of a problem. After our crazy Paris mission, it was back to Ryes. But the Unit was packing up for the Great Move. We trailed out in a very long convoy, having to make way for units rushing through into the swift British advance through northern France and Belgium.

We got lost between Caen and Lisieux, came across a silent and empty road, applied the cigarette packet test, turned off the road—and promptly got blown up by a mine! Clambering out from the overturned jeep, I found my head ringing incessantly but no obvious damage. They shipped the three of us off to an American Field Dressing Station, just in case.

We were kept overnight, as my head cleared, and I was lying there when an American general came round, issuing Purple Heart medals to the wounded. He moved from bed to bed, saluting and declaring 'America is proud of you!' as he handed them over. Both Americans and Russians issued the actual medals—the latter used to walk around clanking! We had to make do with ribbons, as a second-rate power, no doubt.

As he reached my bed and started the routine, I let out a plaintive protest. He paused, stared and then said 'Hell, take it, son. America is proud of you, too!' I cherished that gong for a long time, but in the end swapped it in Versailles for cigarettes from an American who reckoned it would do him a power of good back in Philadelphia.

Out then, breathless with zeal for that sweep through to Brussels and beyond, only to find the Reinforcement Holding Unit had been shunted off to a backwater behind Dieppe, where it looked like settling in for a long siege. Friends back home took to writing at this time—'Good heavens, where are you now? You'll be in Germany in no time,' while I, stuck there, glowered at the deadly familiar tents and the even more deadly potato mountains. We used to spend the free hours playing endless cards with a farmer in his farmhouse. It was the unbreakable Army pastime—and I've hated cards ever since. But at last, the Signals mob were mobilised and we were directed to Versailles, to join the British contingent of SHAEF.

SHAEF, which had an absolutely splendid shoulder flash which we sewed on everything within reach, pyjamas and all, was housed in the Stables of the Palace of Versailles. There was a great, sloping square of cobbles and beyond it, the Palace. It was a surprisingly un-impressive facade—my companion in later years refused to believe it was *The Palace*!

But when you got beyond the front courtyard, as we did from time to time, the full splendours of Louis XIV and Marie Antoinette burst on your eyes: the long formal gardens, the ponds, the little palaces, the statues—the carp, with their ceaselessly moving, contemptuous mouths! The Germans had tried to desecrate the place before leaving and the French were still cleaning up. I remember standing in the Hall of Mirrors, where the Treaty was signed, staring hypnotised at neat piles of human shit which the Germans had left in every room. It was a habit they also cultivated in Russia.

Opposite, across the Square, were the Stables. Two enormous semi-circular sweeps of elegant buildings, punctuated by archways, great and small, with a rabbit-warren of rooms behind and some splendid, spacious chambers upstairs. Behind, a maze of inner courtyards. They were separated by a broad, breathtaking avenue leading to Paris. The two complexes were identical, but one was called Les Grandes Ecuries. Naturally Eisenhower and his merry men were there. The other, Les Petites, was ours—three doors to the right of the main archway, first floor window, to be exact.

I at once had an attack of the horrors. British Signals had taken over most of the real jobs and they worked almost exclusively on the dread teleprinters—whose incomprehensible spirit haunted my whole Army career! After a few days' agony, we at last came to a settlement and I was set to repairing phones and radios just like a bloody American.

Not that I cared. I was happy enough tinkering away in our two floors which served as a workshop. The boys had two ATS girls call in regularly. One, who was nice if raunchy, had a curious on-off affair with one of us and would regale him with tales of the Frenchmen she'd been out with . . . 'What's a French kiss?' he'd mutter morosely . . . But the girls became permanent fixtures. The little one, pleasant, plain, apparently inexperienced, was allotted to me, with strict instructions from Raunchy, who was looking after her, Never To Go Too Far. I didn't either—the one time I tried a tentative kiss, she had hysterics.

So it settled into a regular routine for months on end. Days ran into each other. I can remember almost nothing. There were two sorties, out to Colmar near the Rhine, where I got my first glimpse of the Land of the Boche and up into the wintry Reichswald Forest, where I was terrified out of my wits. But the high point of our official life came near the end of it—8 May 1945, VE Day !

When the Day dawned, a great friend of mine called Shon was deputed to go into Paris to fix a teleprinter. For once, I went with him. He did the job in no time and, with many others, we hung around on the stairs, trying to hear Churchill's broadcast on the radio . . . 'Advance Britannia! God Save the King!'—and out we poured into a Paris seething with jubilant crowds.

It was astonishing to move through those crowds—the bottles of wine, cries of '*Vive l'Angleterre!*' and of course, girls, every one of whom seemed infinitely desirable. We were struck by the relative absence of British soldiers, so we nipped into the British Embassy and stole (well, borrowed) a Union Jack. Then, just the two of us, with the enormous flag between us, started to walk up the Champs Elysees.

It was fantastic. In no time at all, there were huge crowds lining up alongside and behind us. We ended up leading what became a monster demonstration! A long line of office girls, linked arms with us and tramped along singing . . . 'Ees a long vay to Tipperaree'. A little old lady, impeccably dressed, came right up to me to clap furiously in my face. The few British, possibly because they were few, were very popular. So it went on for hours, up and down the Champs Elysees, with cheers, oaths of undying friendship, bottles cracking open all over the place.

We suddenly fell silent as a bus came through carrying people just out of the Nazi camps, still in their striped uniforms. I can see them now, staring impassively out at us, their faces dead pale, strangers at the feast. They never moved a muscle through all the jubilation. This gave us a turn, but shortly afterwards the crowd discovered three Red Army officers in a jeep. They went mad, hoisted them out of the jeep to carry them, laughing and protesting, right up to the Champs Elysees.

Worn out by these patriotic labours, we slumped into the American Rainbow Corner. I'd been there before, notably to hear the Glenn Miller band after they'd lost their leader in the crossing. They were then rather subdued. All I recollect is that they played 'God Save the King' in swing—which provoked a minor diplomatic incident.

This night, though, the joint was heaving to the endless beat of the big bands. Thousands of people were twirling around and singing. Suddenly, out of the dense throng, came a French ATS girl. She really was utterly ravishing, very petite, very dark with flashing, mischievous eyes. And she was giving me that eye! Off I went, in sheer ecstasy, locked in a mad dance with those eyes and that smile . . . till Shon came up and muttered something about the Sergeants' Mess. Funny bugger, Shon.

So I tore myself away from the love of my life down to the Madeleine where the upper windows of the Sergeants' Mess were lined with men all banging their mugs on the placard which stretched the length of the building. They got into a regular rhythm, with people dancing to it. In there, then, to drink ourselves stupid and to lurch for the Versailles truck.

And it was then that Shon, eyeing the couples enlaced together on the grass, all legs and knickers, caught in the truck's headlamps, began to feel sexual frustration. What the hell did he think he'd been doing in Rainbow Corner, I wailed? But there was no point. We were both worn out.

Shon's name was the bane of his life. His father was something Very Big in the Civil Service—Regional Controller Wales or some such title. He was uneasy over his son turned loose in the Army— he had some reason, as I remember! He was something of a Welsh Nationalist and instead of calling his son Something Davies, he had him registered as Sion ab Emrys.

This was agony for Shon. His name inevitably came first on any roster and sergeant after sergeant would get stuck over it. It usually came out as Abybeemyers! And Shon would groan his presence. To ward off Papa, he spun him a yarn that he'd met a very steady, very respectable Welsh boy who would keep him on the straight and narrow. That was me. I bloody nearly collapsed when he told me.

The pay-off came after the war, when I was summoned to Cardiff by a grateful parent. It was in his tall offices in Cathays Park, near the Castle. I was interviewed and taken to lunch. He asked what I wanted to do and looked appalled when I said something about History. 'Young man,' he said earnestly, 'get a Degree in Economics and Come and See Me!' I have often wondered since whether I should have done. God, by now I might be Boss of a Quango, awarding myself a trifling pay increase of £275,000 p.a.!

We lived in the barracks, down a busy road from the Stables, across the Red Ball Expressway and up the hill to an ancient French centre—Camp Satory—a journey we did four times a day for months. Camp Satory in later years was a series of pleasant pedestrian walkways through stately buildings but in our day it was walled off, with French, British and American guards. There were even graffiti in the barracks rooms by prisoners from the Paris Commune of 1871 who had survived the Death March from Paris, when the anthem, the *Internationale* was written—there's tradition for you.

Inside, the camp was a pleasant enough place, with a cinema, a theatre, a Red Shield canteen of the Salvation Army, a library with

Marx, a newspaper centre and innumerable clubs. At one time, I signed on for cross-country running and drama, to keep me up to scratch. We were all mixed up together: French, British and American, with an intense cosmopolitan life all our own.

There were a couple of crises. The Gaullist armies were then mostly black and their colonialism was still rampant. It was about this time that there was an uprising in Algeria—though none of this registered with us. What did register was that the Muslim and African troops in Camp Satory mutinied. There was shooting, with Africans running around waving bayonets and shouting, French soldiers armed to the teeth moving in, the victims carted off in trucks. We were shut up for days in the barracks, in enforced neutrality and considerable apprehension.

Then there was the great American scandal. In the winter, they discovered a gangster ring in the transport department which was hijacking supplies and funnelling them off to the French Black Market. It was highly organised, Mafia style, and well armed. The focus was Camp Satory. The crisis lasted for several days with all sorts of security troops moving in, shots ringing through the walkways, mass arrests.

It precipitated a prolonged famine in cigarettes. The front line got priority, so the Americans with us were starved. For weeks you couldn't get near the Red Shield for the long lines of Americans queueing up to get tins of 50 Players.

But what I remember most was a coy little advert stuck up on an American notice board asking for volunteers for a baseball team. The spirit of Dan Jones the sports master came into its own. I can still remember the shock when I strolled into the canteen and presented myself. They were appalled. Not only a Limey but a shrimp of a Limey at that! But baseball at Cyfarthfa was the one team game I excelled at. With whatever reluctance the Americans felt, after trials I was admitted to the SHAEF Tigers and became one of them, possibly the only Britisher to serve in an American Army baseball team.

So every other Saturday, I'd be pitching and belting the leather with the best of them. It went on in a League, for months, ignoring niceties about seasons. In the end, as we were about to leave for Germany, we staged a farewell ceremony. It was decided to burn our records. My point that this created our own Ashes did not register. So the ritual burning went ahead. For the SHAEF Tigers scored a record unequalled in the annals of baseball, I believe. We never won a single bloody game!

But the real significance of Versailles for me was the French. It began by accident, by my asking if there was room at a table in the cafe which became our nightly haunt, one of many in the street leading up to the Stables. By that time, I was making steady use of the One French Idiom I'd discovered in school—*Je parle francais comme une vache espanol.* It meant literally I speak French like a Spanish cow. I discovered later that it was strictly a *French* idiom. When I used it in Belgium—just after crossing the French border, too—they took it at face value and looked at me as if I were mad. I remember being appalled that a linguistic frontier could be so abrupt. But in France, it won an immediate response, laughter and drinks all round.

It worked again in Versailles. '*Mais,*' they said in unbelieving tones, '*Vous n'etes pas Anglais*!? . . .' Which of course set me off on my customary paean on the Deathless Splendour of Being Welsh. They found relief in the end, by cutting me off and asking me to join them . . . I was with them for the next nine months.

Night after night, I'd rush down to the Street to spend evenings with them; the few British mates who started off coming with me soon gave up. But I went everywhere with them, spending long hours in endless discussions on everything under the sun, going to their cinemas, to their dances, out on their trips around Versailles and the occasional raids ino Paris at weekends, just mooching around the Street. My name, Gwyn, in French was apparently something unprintable which provoked gales of laughter, so Monsieur Taffy it was (to be followed in due course by Herr Taffy and even Tovarich Taffy). In the end, my French was such that people said I talked it like a Parisien with a Marseilles accent! At the time, I took that as a compliment.

Once we went, with great ceremony, to a house where a little old lady was said to make tea 'exactly as the English did'. I sat through this Special Treat as she served up something dreadful and undrinkable and was, of course, Enormously Impressed. They used to come with me on shopping excursions and advise me on what I should buy my young brother back home. I spent Christmas and the New Year with them, in rituals which were incomprehensible. In the Dupuis household, which was our base, they solemnly presented me with a dish with an enormous upturned tureen cover over it. Madame Dupuis whipped it off to reveal a tiny cigarette holder: my Christmas present. I felt then, as I've felt many times since, particularly in southern France, that I'd been born in the wrong place.

I thought of them as French sixth-formers, a very familiar type. I never asked about their dread Baccalaureat, but they were all more or less my age and most of them had jobs. The call-up in France got going slowly and only caught Guy in the end. My best friend was Dede, Andre Deganis, who was sallow and solemn but had a vivid sense of humour. With him I discussed many points of etiquette —particularly on my approach to Charmaine who used to waltz around us all!—but on everything else as well. There was Bernard, who reminded me of Davy Blackwell, solid, firm, a sportsman, a bit tongue-tied but a regular. And there was Guy, like a reasonable Glyn Harris, tall, smooth, with a line in cynicism. He'd had this girl taken away by a British soldier and would sometimes enliven debate with a sudden toast—*A la perte de l'Angleterre*! This would set me off on tortured defence of British honour—with the essential saving grace thrown in: the Ineffable Glory of Being Welsh, on which I started to expound at my customary length until in the end they all rebelled in massive protest. I realise now this may have been Guy's wicked purpose all along!

Dede told me once he'd known a German soldier who'd been still a committed Communist and this seemed to explain a certain reticence about his family. We never went there. Bernard's father used to hint at suspect sympathies: '*Pas collaborationiste, pas du tout!*' he'd exclaim, adding . . . '*main un peu collabo.*' I couldn't follow these shades of meaning and didn't much care.

For the Dupuis household was a magic place. Right on the Red Ball Express highway, it was a laundry, a rambling rabbit-warren of a house with umpteen cupboards. It served as a neighbourhood focus, like our house back home, with the world and his wife calling in. Madame Dupuis, a short, wiry, shrewish-looking but massively good-hearted woman, would preside, forever ironing sheets and shirts. Her daughter Lisette was her spitting likeness, sharing the sheets and shirts, Catholic and deeply puritanical. I loved that household.

Over it presided M. Dupuis, short, tubby and twinkly. He'd take me aside from time to time to issue fatherly advice. Once, as we were about to leave for Germany, he felt compelled to give me strictly private counsel. Shooing them all aside, he took me to a different cafe and over a wine, delivered it, in strict confidence. I had to be very careful with Boche women!

He had a friend who'd been in the French army in Germany after World War I and he'd heard this absolutely authentic story from one of his mates.

He'd noticed that we British moved about unarmed, which struck Versaillese as a sharp contrast to the Germans. This was all well and good, we were among friends. But *les Boches*! Ah, that was very different! I was to watch out in particular for their women. German women, he assured me, would make up to you like mad, take you home and into their bed. But once you were stretched out there, awaiting the ultimate ecstacy, they'd make an excuse, slip into the bathroom and strap on a pair of enormous spurs. Then, just at the moment when you lost control in orgasm, up would go their legs and down would come the spurs, driven right into your back, so that you expired on the spot like a French Bishop in a brothel.

I had difficulty keeping a straight face at the time and the story has seemed extremely risible ever since. Yet in Germany I did occasionally catch myself suspiciously eyeing the heels of forward young women.

Not long after the War, in 1948 in fact, I was coming back from Jugoslavia and made a point of going out to Versailles and the Street. We were in the very cafe when M. Dupuis came in, short and plump and smiling as always. I just couldn't talk to him. He'd have without doubt re-introduced me to the old gang—and I couldn't face it. It was as if I felt instinctively that these two worlds could not mix. They should not mix. My memories of Versailles, like everything else in the Army, had to be kept to one side. It was as if they were not wholly real. That damned newsreel effect again— which I now realise has afflicted me throughout my life and in more than Army memories.

There was one moment, though, when my two worlds in Versailles came together in the Cause—which I shared with my French friends. The key was the ritual known in SHAEF as Burning The Secret Waste. All those ATS girls in all those rooms, at all those teleprinters were taking down, among other things, Top Secret memos, instructions, background briefings. The disposal of the spare copies was clearly a matter of crucial significance. It had to be the function of Responsible People—such as the technical Sergeants of the Signals Corps.

So, in our time off, we would religiously march into long, high-ceilinged rooms full of ATS girls at their teleprinters. They all seemed incredibly, suspiciously attractive—Officers, for the use of, clearly! We'd scrabble about under their desks, between those gorgeous legs, groping around for their special bins with the secret material. It was rather enjoyable.

I remember one moment vividly. I was scrambling around as usual, with a particularly recalcitrant set of records, trying to avoid contact with those breath-taking legs, when a charming face appeared upside down under the edge of the desk and a beautifully-modulated voice said—'You disgusting little Welsh toad! Why don't you get back to the barracks and wank!'

I stood up, flushed, banging my head and leg on the desk, drew myself up to my full five foot, and prepared to defend myself. Thinking better of it, I mustered my self-command and stalked off, in great dignity, with reams of Top Secret Waste trailing in my wake.

It was down then, to a furnace in one of the courtyards, where we'd formally burn the lot. We read them first, of course. We'd spend hours going through secret telegrams from everywhere, revelling in our new-found knowledge even though half of it was incomprehenisble. I remember once when great tomes came through, multiple volumes of detailed surveys of the Balkan countries, compiled for some obscure reason, by the Royal Navy. Albania alone merited four volumes, so God knows how much Jugoslavia took. They were fascinating. I believe some of them formed the basis of some Cambridge University Press publications after the war. A mate of mine became quite passionate over it. He was going to collect the lot, to make himself a Balkan expert after the war.

It was here that my network of French families came in. I smuggled out many a volume to be stored in the capacious cupboards of the Dupuis family. Those resources were soon to be put to more immediate use.

For we were there when secret messages started to come through about the British role in newly-liberated Greece. It was an appalling story. The British, widely welcomed, ran into the major Greek resistance movement led by ELAS, a communist-led coalition. We did not know it then, but Stalin had 'handed over' Greece to Britain, with America later taking over. This meant delivering it to Churchill with his monarchist obsessions. The process could be traced almost day by day in the Secret correspondence, a process of procrastination, deceit, delay, until the royalist forces could be mobilised, including the horrible Security Battalions who had collaborated with the Nazis and made a habit of tying severed heads to their saddles. It ended with a full-scale British army assault on ELAS in the hopeless cause of the lousy Greek monarchy, which had family ties, of course, with our own. It led on into the long and miserable civil war which dragged on for years. A similar process was also visible at the same time, on a less dramatic scale, in Belgium. It won the approval of Labour no less than Tory politicians in government.

There was a terrible outcry at home, I remember, and most of us were seized with a frightful rage. Natural selection singled out three of us, all Soldiers of the International. We decided to Do

Something. So I mobilised the Dupuis family and others, swore them to secrecy and began to smuggle out selected Secret Waste to be stored with them against The Day. We decided to do a Kim Philby, betray our country and its lousy class-ridden hypocrisy in the cause of humanity and the International. Stalin's own hypocrisy was mercifully hidden from us. We would hand this material over to the Russians who, we assumed, would be in Paris.

It might have come to nothing, though, if we hadn't all gone to the cinema, to see Betty Grable, I think. There was, with it, a dreadful British Gaumont newsreel on show. The Gaumont British newsreels were always horrible but this one was on the troubles in Greece. It was so sickeningly celebratory that we were driven mad. Churchill had visited Athens about that time and the story we heard was that, half-drunk, he had himself driven about the place, brandishing pistols and shouting 'Come on out ELAS! Come out and fight!' Good God, where did he think he was—Tonypandy?

We decided The Day had come. So over a few days's careful planning, with much co-ordination between French households, we Sergeants Three descended on the central depot, chez M. and Mme. Dupuis, collected all the material in two huge black bags and brought a small trolley to wheel them in. So equipped, we set off for Paris.

I like to think now we went straight through the Palace of Versailles. I'm not sure, but it would have been great if we had —trundling our load past all those statues of coy females, the grandiose vistas, the carp with their mouths moving endlessly like so many lying bastards of Labour and Tory ministers.

Out certainly then—into the train. We stood there with our load, trying to look nonchalant, while French passengers stared curiously at us. Out at Paris. Whenever an American Military Police patrol went by, we'd freeze, feigning a fixed interest in some landmark and trying to distance ourselves from our ungainly burden with its inadequate trolley.

God, we must have spent hours trundling that load through

Paris, searching the Embassy quarter, embarrassing all and sundry with our questions, up and down past all those lovely bridges, down and up again. Whenever you wanted bloody Russians, you could never find them!

In the end, exhausted after many fruitless hours, we slumped into a cafe in the Champs Elysees. In our bitterness and fatigue, we spotted salvation. He was slumped there, completely drunk. He had a big bush hat on. It did not actually have corks dangling from it, but he was an Australian and, we gathered with some difficulty, a journalist. Harangues produced no visible effect. So after a hurried consultation, we dumped the lot on him and fled, capering and whooping right down the Champs Elysees.

At least, we'd tried to do our duty as Soldiers of the International!

It wasn't until after the war that I learned that Stalin had abolished the Third International in 1943.

DOORBELLS IN BRUSSELS

'Ah Christ, Taffy,' said Jock morosely, humped over the wheel, 'What's a shag? What is it, eh? . . . a bloody shower, a bloody beer . . .a bloody shag, Christ, who cares? . . . It's nothing . . . Ugh! . . . Balls! . . .' and he spat out of the window, in some obscure rage.

This was just after he'd curtly rebuffed two gorgeous German girls who had tried to get a lift on the truck, one of them hitching her breasts right through the window. If there was mass rape in the Russian zone of Germany, so there was in ours: only the victims changed.

Jock slumped into silence. I sensed some hurt in him and shut up. So it went on, the two of us slumped in silence in the cab of the truck as it thundered endlessly on, along endless roads with their endless crowds of shuffling and displaced people: Germans, French, Dutch, Poles, Jugoslavs, God knows who. It looked as though the whole of Europe was on the move, going home, going somewhere, going anywhere . . . It was that newsreel effect, again; my sense of pity seemed to have dried up. I no longer remember the faces of the people, just the endless smell of petrol and sweat in my nostrils, the endless river passing on our left, every bridge blown, every town a ruin. And, now and then, a stop to brew up for us and our passengers—a great mound of dirt with half a jerrican of petrol sloshed over it, a match, a rush into the explosion with mess-tins and instant tea!

We were heading north from Frankfurt along the Rhine towards Belgium in that stunning summer of 1945. At the end of the War, SHAEF packed up and moved to Frankfurt. I remember the long convoys trundling through Metz to my first German town, Saarbrucken, which was an utterly empty shell, past women holding out their children as a pledge of harmlessness, into Frankfurt which I don't remember at all, except that, for a ruin, it seemed vaguely 'modern'. We were housed in a great, empty hangar. Almost at once Jock came to me to announce that he had to drive three of our people to the old familiar Reinforcement Holding Unit in Bruges in Belgium and had chosen me as his 'guard'.

Since he was a six foot plus Glaswegian who'd been something in the gangs and I was a five foot and a fart Mam's Boy, this had its comic quality. But in fact we were old friends. (I always seemed to end up with six foot truck-drivers, though I was unaware of any psychological implications.) Once, on a raid out from Versailles, we had blundered with the crew into the Germans in the Reichswald Forest—a terrifying predicament from which Jock extricated us —and we'd been mates ever since.

On the road north, he elaborated on his long-term schemes. We were to form a patnership of Brain and Brawns. I was to supply the Brains in the form of my fractured French. The intention was that I should engage a *gendarme* in friendly chit-chat, while Jock sneaked up behind him, broke his neck and collared his pistol—which would do him no end of good in his post-war Glasgow career. We spent the hours indulging in fantasies of the untold wealth the Plan would bring in, culminating in very early retirement on the Cote d'Azur (the Costa del Sol was nowhere in mind, then).

More immediately, he planned to break the truck down at Brussels, so that we could have a spell in the fleshpots. Cheered by this prospect, we drove on, into night and Bruges where we delivered our cargo. Nearly forty years later, I visited Bruges, which is hailed as the Gem of Flanders. It was certainly a very pretty town, with good architecture and pleasing canals, in the middle of a fearfully dull and flat Flemish landscape, though its museums promised more than they performed. At the time, I hardly saw it, or Ghent, but after much fiddling under the bonnet, we finally achieved our breakdown in the outskirts of Brussels. The SHAEF detachment there duly rescued us and put us up while the truck was repaired.

There followed about ten days' Life of Riley. We'd go our separate ways during the day and meet up in the evening at a cafe which was actually called *At the Two Maggots*. I can't recollect much of Brussels now, other than the Manneken-Pis and the palaces but I had an enjoyable time pottering around, taking drinks in odd cafes, chatting people up in my rectified (non-idiomatic) sixth-form-cum-'Marseilles' French.

Cards were all the rage at base and I was caught up in endless games of pontoon. Once, by three in the morning, I was in debt to the tune of £3,000 (a strictly civilian experience since) but by eight, was £3-10s in the clear! Not that it mattered: all IOUs were ceremonially destroyed at first light. Just as well, otherwise most of the British garrison in Brussels would have been paupers and a handful millionaires. This was before Thatcher, of course.

It was the time of the General Election at home and the fact that I, too young to vote, was haranguing everyone within reach, was the subject of much ribald mirth. I vividly remember the day the result was announced. An officer came in, leapt on the table and declared that, at long last, a Labour Goverment With A Proper Majority had been elected. It was the New Dawn. We all roared 'The Red Flag'. Some of us went on into 'The Internationale'. The officer joined us in both. A People's Army, *sans doute*!

The nights, however, were a strain. The first night I reached *The Two Maggots* at the appointed time only to hear a tremendous din inside and then Jock came flying out the door, propelled by about six bruisers, it seemed, to squat in the street and curse. I pushed in and demanded, in my best British style, to know what alleged crime my mate had been accused of, by a bunch of foresworn perjurers, no doubt. 'Son,' said a drunken American, lurching up off the floor, 'we don't hit women where I come from.' Irritated beyond words, I snarled back, 'No more do we, buster,' and was promptly engaged in a brawl-cum-slanging match, in defence of male honour, as we then somewhat ludicrously defined it. In the end, the landlady, moved perhaps by pity, intervened and ultimately secured peace in our time all round, with Jock re-admitted amid solemn handshakes and pledges of total human solidarity.

That was just the beginning. Jock's vision of our joint assault on a *gendarme* suddenly assumed a grotesque and terrifying reality. Night after night, wounded by my repeated evasions of my responsibility to the Partnership, he'd squat in his appointed place and howl. When I eventually stalked off, he let out a yell— 'Doan leave me, Taff! Taff! doan leave! . . . I didn't leave you, did I?' Which could not be denied. So it was, shuffling about in despair in the small hours in one corner of a deserted Brussels, that I came across THE DOORBELLS.

It was a short street near the *Two Maggots*. I was loafing there at a complete loss when I suddenly spotted the bell-push. But what a bell-push! Rather it was a bell-pull. A splendid thing, lavishly engraved, set deep in the door, with an elaborate handle. There was even a kind of carved pad for your free hand. I'd never seen anything like it. 'Jock, Jock!' I shouted, 'Look at this!' When he failed to respond, I demonstrated it. My hand rammed firmly against the pad, I lugged that bell-pull out as if my life depended on it and was rewarded with a terrific clamour within. I immediately scuttled round the corner, as the house lit up and people in dressing-gowns wandered aimlessly about, questioning each other. If they made anything of a soldier slumped in the gutter, it did not register. I meanwhile was in ecstasies of mad laughter.

That liberated us. Night after night, we'd take opposite sides of the street and, at a given signal, walk swiftly and systematically down it, pulling those bells in a delirium of delight, to collapse around the corner in gales of hysterical laughter as the street came alive with lights, dressing gowns and angry voices.

We were fools. It never entered our drunken heads that anyone would complain. Until one night, we'd hardly begun before blinding lights appeared from nowhere and two sets of *gendarmes*, pistols drawn, advanced down the street towards us. I caught a glimpse of Jock's mad eye on the pistols in the torchlight and felt panic welling up. But nothing happened. When they saw what we were, they stopped dead. '*Merde*,' said one and they sent for the Military Police.

We must have been a sight. I was wearing an American combat jacket festooned with Soviet and Resistance badges, Jock sported a decrepit Army jersey with favours from sundry liberated females all over it. The waggon came screeching up and three M.P.s got out of it and strolled over. They towered there like walking War Memorials.

'Hello,' said one in menacing tones. 'What's all this, then? Boys having a bit of fun, are we?'

Desperate, I muttered a few words of the Lord's Prayer in Welsh and said 'Me Pole! . . . Pole!' and laughed ingratiatingly. There was a pause.

'Oh yes,' said one of them. 'What part of Poland you from? I'm from Pontypridd myself.' Another pause. He gestured— 'Hitch your Taff arse into that waggon.' I did so with alacrity. They threw Jock in.

We scudded through the night to a prison somewhere. Humped out and through documentation, we were marched into a round room, with a thick central pillar and sat on a bench around the wall.

Around the dimly lit room, we could make out several humped figures. They were all manacled. The ones on the central bench around the pillar were shackled to it as well.

'What happened to the bitch?', a voice resumed its questioning from the pillar, 'You should've had her guts out.' The man addressed swivelled his flat, venomous eyes, blank as a toad's, back to his companion. 'It was him I wanted. I could see his arse going out the window, his bloody pants going all ways. Got him at the foot of the stairs. That bastard'll have trouble finding his prick when he wants it . . .'

There was a charged silence. Toad-eyes turned his blank stare round the room . . . 'What are you in for? . . . yes, you, cows' piss?' Answers were extracted like rotten teeth . . . mayhem . . . rape, robbery . . . Silence . . . Then the eyes turned on me— 'Hey, you! Shortarse! What did they get you for, poof?'

I couldn't speak. A terrible paralysis seized Jock and myself.

Toad-eyes spat. It landed between my feet. I started to shuffle them closer, caught those eyes on me and froze.

'I didn't catch what you said' . . . He was remorseless.

Then the M.P. at the door spoke . . . 'These,' he gestured grandly, 'these are real hard cases. They're in for ringing doorbells.'

RUSSIANS AND OTHERS

That Brussels jail was a turning point. After a suitable punishment—whitewashing a kitchen, perched on incredibly long and shaky ladders high above bowls of boiling fat, towards which we'd occasionally skid in heart-stopping manner—we returned to Frankfurt, to find nobody there!

SHAEF had split up and the British contingent had gone on leave. We finally hitched a lift on an American Dakota without seats. Spinning around the hull like peas, we'd hang on to the nearest support and stare out of the windows at the battered Rhine flowing by. On the way back, I was redirected on Paddington platform and emerged in the Gare St. Lazare in Paris in the rain. Jock I never saw again.

The British component of SHAEF had come all the way back, to be housed in the grounds of a chateau at Fontainebleau. We were in tents around the chateau, which had been a Gestapo centre. It had a lake with boats and we idled through the summer days. We were there when news came through of the Atom Bombs on Hiroshima and Nagasaki. Our first reaction was joy—we had escaped Burma, we thought. There was some sense of a new and devastating weapon, but I cannot say we felt we were entering a new era. At the time, we thought of it as an incredibly powerful bomb, but a bomb nonetheless. It was some time after VJ Day in August that we finally moved up to Germany. We went north, through the France familiar to us from books, cinemas and family memories.

We moved through the First World War battlefields and at Corbie on the Somme, where we stayed a night. I was making great headway with a bunch of sixth-form girls in a cafe when my attention was distracted by a display of some old photographs of British Army units stationed at Corbie during the First War. Among them was my father! I wondered uneasily whether my son might have the same experience in the Third.

We finally reached HQ at Bad Oeynhausen and settled at Minden. There followed for me the usual chaos of half-understood jobs in a number of sorties that left no memory I wished to cherish. There were a few exceptions. We went down to the Rhine near Iserlohn to install the Rhine Army Telephone Exchange. Here at least I could manage to pull wires through the contacts and seal them . . . a process enlivened by The Singer. He had a reasonable voice but transcendent ambitions—and a wide command of scurrilous but often witty Army ditties. But what he concentrated on, with a kind of dedicated ferocity, were to us rather obscure folksongs (we were without benefit of Peter Pears, of course).

> O Soldier, soldier, won't you marry me
> With your musket, fife and drum . . .

He'd carol loudly, beating time as he worked, and on into the catalogue of services offered by an optimistic female.

> So up she went, to her grandfather's chest
> And brought him a coat of the very, very best.
> And the soldier put it on . . .

So it echoed around the mushrooming Exchange and we were expected to join in the chorus (if we could find it).

It echoed right through my 20th birthday party on the banks of the Rhine as we gloomily distributed the ruins of a cake sent by my mother which had fallen apart in the post.

> O no, sweet maid, I cannot marry thee!
> For I have a wife at home.

It echoed even through Berlin, where we were given a few days' leave as a reward for finishing the Exchange ahead of time. I wish I could say that Berlin in 1945 was a memorable experience, but in truth I've forgotten most of it. What I recollect is an ocean of ruins alive with an ant-like humanity. The Singer was a great hit with the famous Berlin cockney women, who were clearing away the rubble, pushing huge wheelbarrows inscribed 'No time for love!' and indulging in racy badinage.

66

They seemed incredibly anarchic and cheerful, joining in the litany of the Soldier and adding no doubt unprintable comments of their own.

The Russians in Berlin, though, were something else and strained my already weakening loyalties to the utmost. We wandered into the Eastern Zone and met unremitting enmity at every step, ferocious glares from sallow and pockmarked soldiers, above all from their officers who all seemed squat and fat with little pig's eyes. We moved towards their great War Memorial, already up, but were stopped in our tracks as the sentry made a vaguely hostile move with his sub-machine gun.

They'd opened a brand-new bookshop just inside the Zone (though there was no Iron Curtain as yet) which I'd have thought was a propaganda bonus. When I saw the display in the window, I was delighted. It was my kind of reading. There in the middle was a book by David Williams, the man who was to become my professor at Aberystwyth, on the Chartist march on Newport in 1839, which had been published the year war broke out. Their supply lines must have been good. David Williams, though, was distinctly unhappy when I told him about it some years later.

But as soon as I entered the shop, all agog, one of their pig-eyed officers who had been glaring at us outside gave a shout which brought a poor Russian squaddie at the double, while he installed himself in the shop to glare with manic ferocity at our every move. The shop assistant was crippled with embarrassment. As I bought the David Williams book, having abandoned all hope of browsing through the shelves, the officer made a move as if to intervene but did not. As we left, he followed us out, still glaring at us, and sent his dumb soldier to shepherd us menacingly clean out of his precious Zone.

This left such a taste that I was quite unprepared for a very different encounter with Russians which followed almost at once. A group of us were despatched, across what became the Zonal border, to a place near Madgeburg, to help install a cable cellar. We ran straight into a Red Army detachment which was clearly a front-line unit, unlike the then garrison of Berlin.

They gave us an uproarious welcome and made us totally at home. They'd join in our 'technical' operations, offering profuse advice in their own language or rather languages, took us in to their all-night parties round a bonfire, swapped drinks, caps, jackets, badges and all sorts of stuff. We handed over most of our watches in dubious exchanges. We didn't give a damn, for these were 'Russians' as we'd known them from a distance. We were there when a mobile film unit came and I first learned that not all Russian film makers were Eisensteins! It was a cowboys and Indians yarn, with the glorious Red Army as the US Cavalry coming to the rescue of unimaginably noble and heroic partisans (with, of course, a comedy duo thrown in). It was an experience repeated almost identically in Jugoslavia a few years later.

German women were strolling around, arm in arm with them, to our surprise, but they had their own women soldiers with them. These were technically I believe traffic policewomen. They were striking Ukrainian girls, buxom but attractive, with a lively sense of humour, blonde hair and black eyebrows. They'd be the star turn in the sing-songs around the bonfire at night, when there was a dance which I realised later was like the Jugoslav *kolo*, sung for our benefit, I believe, full of references to Churchill which were beyond us, perhaps mercifully. But they also sang war songs, one of which, '*Krivoi Rog*', was to haunt me to this day.

I met Vlado, much my own age. He'd been a student during the war in Kiev, aiming to be a doctor. He'd shared the horrors of the war but also its glories. If it's not too much of a contradiction, he was liberal minded but a patriot. In our pidgin German, we'd swap our dreams of a post-war utopia of friendship. It got so close that we once climbed a hill nearby and mingled our blood, swearing never to go to war with each other throughout our lives. These Boy Scout hopes soon seemed ridiculous, but what the hell, in 1945 it was as well to Be Prepared.

One night round the bonfire, I was suddenly struck by a face across the fire. It was that of someone from the Soviet Far East;

slant-eyed, long hair, almost in a pigtail, with a thin moustache pencilled in. He looked the spitting image of my boyhood nightmares of Dr Fu Manchu! With a quavering finger I pointed him out to Yuri. He turned out to be a Baptist missionary in Central Asia who was a dedicated supporter of Stalin. Communisim was never the same again.

After this unhinging experience came another, this time quintessentially *British*. Some of us were suddenly told we were to form part of a Telecommunication Specialist Section with a particular Mission. There were six of them, it seems; one had gone to Chiang Kai Shek in Chungking, another had been dropped to Tito in wartime Jugoslavia. What breathtaking Mission we were to enjoy was still a secret.

It was the oddest unit I have ever been in. So far as I could tell, Bill Brown my mate, another truck-driver and I were among the few 'normal' soldiers among them. They flew out a whole detachment from England. Most of them were GPO engineers from Nottingham and thereabouts who'd been given six weeks' basic training and then deployed. They were in fact a good bunch and my first real introduction to the ethos of the Royal Signals which was virtually interchangeable with the GPO. There was a great deal of Post Office talk about how their prospects of promotion would be affected by this peculiar form of Army Service.

No sooner had they all arrived and been given the rank of Corporal, than they were told to draw lots to choose two Sergeants. No sooner was this done, than the two Elect decided to establish a separate Sergeants' Mess!

This stupefying exercise in Deathless British Tradition was brought crashing when Bill Brown threatened to cut off the supply of black market chickens and eggs from German farms. It was while such struggles for power were being fought that we learned at last what our particular Mission was to be: it was to take over Hannover Repeater Station, described grandly as the Crewe Junction of German telecommunications.

MAKING A STAND IN HANNOVER

Hannover looked like another giant ruin but wasn't. By this time, these ubiquitous ruins, shocking in their stark nakedness, were haunting me. I was driven to poetry again— 'Stars and ruins weave for us the pattern of our age . . .' I began. Unfortunately, as usual, it was much more difficult to follow up the first lines. Even more unfortunately, news of this strictly private enterprise leaked out. I was promptly dubbed The Poet and called on for verse on every possible occasion, like a Laureate.

But, for the first time in the Army, I was absolutely on top of the work; I could do it! I enjoyed it hugely, moving around the Repeater Station which boosted signals in all directions. A particular pleasure were the New Circuits, usually handled during night shifts. It was sheer joy to trace the signals from their entry point right through every connection in the place, correcting faults where necessary, to see them out to Minden or wherever and on to London, signing the necessary forms with a flourish. For the first time in the Army, I felt whole.

I do not know what happened to the Specialist Section; it just vanished. We were a Line of Communication unit in 30 Corps, under General Brian Horrocks who was very popular. The Corps badge was the Wild or, *chez nous*, the Randy Boar. Its governing feature was the Boar's penis on which truck painters would exercise their fevered imagination, until Corps HQ finally sent out a memo—'The Boar's private parts will be reduced to normal proportions immediately!'

Hannover, on closer inspection, nursed islands of unscathed buildings in the sea of ruins. One was our billet, a newly-built secondary school in a suburb; another was the Repeater Station itself, just around the corner from the great square in front of the Bahnhof, where the half-ruined railway station was very busy, disgorging thousands of people with mountains of baggage into the trolley-buses. The Repeater Station (Verstarker Amt) was also modern, approached by a flight of steps, through glass doors, intact, up another flight into the main Station area. It was in truth a key point between Berlin and London and we, taking over what was left of the German staff, had it operative in no time.

Nearly all the boys had been GPO engineers with a certain nous. They used to pull out U-links in the evening, talk to the Army PX in London, staffed by old mates, and get transferred to the civilian exchange to indulge in long, free phone talks with their wives and God wot. Unfortunately, nobody I knew had a phone. Once, Fred Turton pulled out a U-link, only to be called away to another job. Just as well, for he'd have been chatting up whoever Field Marshal Montgomery was talking to at the time! There was a fearful rocket after that; the Station hummed with officers and all VIP lines through were marked with red paint. We were regularly the target of official visits of all kinds. We'd be shunted off to a corner with the German staff, mouthing subversive and bilingual comment, as the Brass and Friends, Mistresses and Hangers-On moved around in blank comprehension.

It was in Hannover that I was fully inducted into the spirit of the Royal Corps of Signals. 'You're not a bloody soldier,' a man told me once. 'You're in the Signals, the bloody gentlemen of the British Army!' Still, REME (Royal Electrical and Mechanical Engineers) were even worse.

Our regimental march was 'Begone, Dull Care!' which, at various parades, blared out across the German countryside, with a *sotto voce* chorus supplying our own unorthodox versions. Our emblem was Mercury, Messenger of the Gods—Jimmy—with his motto *Certo Cito*, Swiftsure.

> Ashes to ashes, Dust to Dust,
> Certo Cito, Shit or Bust.

The billet (which, *mirabile dictu*, had beds, not bunks) echoed to in-jokes about a decibel being one-tenth of a Clang and long, elaborate and filthy verses, taken up seriatim in part-song and

71

chorus, full of technical data. At night, as we lay there, worn out from endless games of chess (which had seized every man of us by the throat) a sepulchral voice would loom out of the dark—

'And the Lord said unto Moses,

It tickles'

From another corner, came yet another graveyard voice—

'And Moses said,

What tickles?'

Came the reply—'Testicles' and the whole billet would chorus —'And the drinks were on Moses'—and so on into an infinity of variation, followed up by apparently inexhaustible songs, incredibly lewd and politically incorrect but which I found excruciatingly funny, particularly since the entire mob would take them up, in part song, solo tremolo and even varieties of Gregorian Chant! The experience proved unforgettable (and examples could be provided)!

I suppose, for the first time, I knew what *esprit de corps* meant, at least in our strictly unofficial version. Imagine our horror, then, when we were abruptly informed that the Royal Corps was to be promoted to a Regiment in full cavalry style. They gave us a new regimental march which we listened to in sullen silence; not much scope for various dull cares to begone there! All the ranks changed, Signalmen became Troopers and so on. Some officers started sporting jodhpurs, which sat uneasily with GPO spirits and there was even a fearful rumour that we were to be issued with spurs.

I don't know what happened to the Royal Signals Regiment. The last I knew of the familiar bunch, it was still the same old Royal Corps of Signals and its march was still 'Begone, Dull Care' in all its infinite variety. *Gott sei danke*! to borrow a phrase from our assistants.

I made friends there I was to cherish. Apart from Bill Brown the driver, there was Johnny, a tall, fair Englishman who'd been *Readers Digest* representative and Boy Chess Champion of the Southern Counties. He had a passion for Gilbert and Sullivan, and since this did not go well with the tastes of the billet with its everlasting radios, he used to regale with us with 'Tit Willow' on our many walks. It was a taste shared by another companion, a very solid, pipe-smoking English moderate, known as Sutton Coldfield, who made it his job to tame my enthusiasms. But there were hosts of them, from Geordie, not a word of whose speech could I understand, to Jock, a Scotsman who was a model of affability off-duty, but who in the Station became fanatical, rushing around with sweat dropping from the end of his nose.

We went everywhere together, to the beloved Red Shield canteen on the banks of a lake nearby which offered everything from boats, telephones, chess-boards, tins of Players cigarettes, chocolates, to a friendly shoulder to weep on; you name it. The Red Shield canteens run by the Salvation Army were universally popular. They cropped up everywhere, in the most unlikely and dangerous places. Storm that blockhouse like Errol Flynn, was the cry. There may not be a blonde in there but there's bound to be a Sally Army lady dishing out the tea. I still, like most of us, have a very soft spot for them.

We saw Marlene Dietrich once. She didn't do much, just graced the show with her presence, but she insisted on us witnessing her latest skill—playing a saw between her legs like a fiddle! She coyly hitched her skirt up about two inches while the Americans went mad and then she solemnly played the saw. It took me some time to recover.

Another time, we took a break from the endless Glenn Miller and the endless cinema, to make a rare visit to an ENSA show. We were drawn by the belly-dancer listed but instead became hooked on an Army comedian whose name was Frankie Howard.

We used to go on jaunts in Bill's truck. Once in Brunswick, a miraculously preserved place, an enterprising character had brought out leaflets for the tourists, 1946 variety—'And so we come to the Potsdammer Platz, where, diurnally, the pigeons flatter down to gain their customary foodings'. He must have prospered under Adenauer!

Strengthened by this experience, no doubt, four of us went to spend a month at the College of the Rhine Army in Gottingen. We saw where Bismarck used to plunge into the river in the small hours (which may be one explanation) and engaged in endless debate on everything under the sun. We heard a talk from the officer who had interrogated Himmler, who issued warnings about a German Resistance movement in the making, called the Werewolves. He'd exercised his trained mind on some of the German students at Gottingen, who took to greeting each other — 'Acht! Acht!' This, he worked out, was the eighth letter in the alphabet—H.H!—i.e. Heil Hitler! We witnessed no further manifestations of the indomitable Teutonic spirit.

What had possessed us all was the Great Chess Mania. Johnny, fed up with being alone, started to teach us chess. It spread like wildfire. In the end, in a billet of 32 men, there'd be 16 games going on simultaneously. I used to gut tomes on the subject, became frightfully learned on the Openings. I used to lie awake at night, unable to sleep, with a ghostly chess-board in front of my eyes. The Red Shield had to order chess-boards for us and games went on in every spare moment. In the end, they invaded the Station itself.

We set up a Chess League along the network; our great rival, I remember, was Munster. And it was here our Germans came in. We set up the board in mid-Station and everybody would be consulted over the Next Move. Our Germans gradually became involved until in the end they were as fanatical as we were.

This was the only time, in my experience, outside the clinically sexual, that barriers between us and the Germans came down. For once, they ceased to be anonymous masses out there. Human beings could emerge from their sullen ranks. In the end, we were in mutual dependence, with supplies from the Naafi and the American PX being funnelled to them in return for their often unconscious services. When we had to say goodbye, after many months, it was quite a wrench.

The experience was not wholly re-assuring. Unfortunately their chief spokesperson was an icy, constipated woman of a certain age, with a remarkably good command of English. Where she got it from, she'd never reveal. So far as she was concerned, the world began in May 1945 when the War ended. She would not hear a word about anything earlier. She made it her job to be Our Conscience. She Criticized!

'Herr Taffy!'—her voice at my shoulder was strained in disbelief. It was an all-too-familiar fifty-year old voice, reminding me of my Aunt Rachel, undeviating in its rectitude. 'Herr Taffy! How can an adult and civilised nation produce a newspaper like this?' And with a contemptuous disregard of her history which had produced so many gems like *Die Sturmer*, she slammed the *Daily Mirror* on the desk.

She was never a Nazi. None of them ever had been, of course, but she claimed to have been a Liberal. Good God, what had their Conservatives been like? In fact, we had a living specimen before our eyes. He was old, probably over the retirement age; he made a fearful ritual out of the most routine job. Slow, deliberate in speech, maddening in his carefully weighed sentiments, he would declare in loud, limited but impeccable English that Germany had been going to the dogs ever since Bismarck. Who were we to disagree? Particularly with a communal grandfather who was painfully teaching himself our language, favouring the longest words he could possibly find.

There was a streak in him, though. They had all been marched off to Belsen Camp after we took Hannover, presumably as an exercise in Further Education, and the experience rankled. The old man took to leaving massive illustrated tomes from the Kaiser's time about the place, all dedicated to pillorying the British Empire and its camps for Boers. I have a memory of one called, I think *Die Rauptreich*, which displayed shapely young women with nothing on spreadeagled before brutally licentious Tommies—which provoked a lot of unreconstructed mirth. But how could one resist him? 'Herr Taffy,' he declared to me once, in his deafening version of *sotto voce*—'I have an Irresistible Predilection for The Tobacco' . . . One more for the Naafi and PX list. These were our Germans, after all.

A younger one, Hans, however, couldn't give a damn what his English was like. He'd been the equivalent of our GPO engineers and continued the job in uniform. Czechoslovakia had been

O.K. At least they kept quiet. Poland was worse, they kept shooting at you! But worse by far had been Jugoslavia. Never a dull moment, Boom! Boom! all day long . . . 'Barbarians!' he'd declaim, his watery eyes gleaming . . . 'God in Heaven, Herr Taffy! Never have I seen such barbarism!' We'd argue for hours, particularly since he claimed to have been a Social Democrat and I recognised the type.

With him, I had two memorable experiences. He took me to hear Kurt Schumacher speak on the Bahnhof square at night. He was the Socialist leader who'd spent years in Nazi camps. The square was packed, without lights, but with scores of men carrying burning torches. And beyond their glare, against the shadowy ruins, the old man, for his years in the Camps had aged him, was up there on the platform: only one eye and one arm and God knows what else after they'd done with him. There was always the same beautiful young woman by his side and there was always the same harsh, ranting voice, spewing out hatred of Adenauer, the Communists, the Allies and summoning up the ghosts of a long dead German Socialism. Every so often the crowd would break into chants of 'Kurt! Kurt! Schumacher! Schumacher!', lifting their torches in ritual honour. He was One of Us, of course, but the torches and the chants made me hot and uneasy. I can still see poor old Hans now, his eyes taking on an unaccustomed mania as he beat the air with his flaming torch.

The other was more congenial. He rushed on to me in the Station once, crying in desperation—'Herr Taffy—gwmmi! gwmmi! GWMMI!' I didn't know what he was on about. 'GWMMI!' he cried in tones of absolute agony, oblivious to the tortures he was inflicting on his allegedly Liberal fellow-country-woman. 'Gwmmi!' he sobbed as he sank at last to his knees. 'Good God!' I thought, 'can a man get this desperate for gum?' I rushed out as soon as I was free and re-entered in triumph, bearing the biggest box of chewing-gum I'd ever seen (from the Americans of course). Hans let out a bone-chilling cry . . . 'Ach! Gott!' he howled as he hurled the carton right across the Station. It was French letters he was after.

Then there was Rosa who had a secretarial job with the Germans. She was not exactly pretty, more what the French call *jolie-laide*, but charming. We took to each other at once. She had that uneasy blend of respectability and merriment which I remembered from home. I used to feel she was not German at all, a sentiment she apparently reciprocated because she told me once that, after meeting us, she could never marry a German. We were the bloody gentlemen of the British Army, of course.

She was obviously not like her close friend who apparently fell for one of my mates but, because of his appearance, feared he was Jewish despite his denials and suffered appalling agonies of conscience which she communicated to everyone within reach. I could have throttled her.

But Rosa took me everywhere in Hannover and around. We'd travel on the trolley-buses and trams which were running again, when the pasty, expressionless faces of the Germans and the pervading smell of their *ersatz* soap nauseated me; to a beer-cellar where rank young men stared at us warily and sometimes burst into raucous drinking songs, slamming their oversized tankards on the tables. I had to be re-assured that the songs were harmless.

She even took me home once to an estate of flats which had survived in the suburbs. Her parents disapproved. Nazis might have been deplorable but I was still an Enemy of the Heimat. I ran into them as they were going out, tall, shabby and respectable. We exchanged a few formal words as they left, presumably to tramp for hours around ruined streets. On my way home, some youths skulked around and threw stones at me.

Rosa took me to my first opera, in the gracious palace of Herrenhaus nearby. I'd never seen one before but it was to become the sporadic habit of a lifetime. It was *Carmen*, still my favourite (popular, of course). I had not yet, however, mastered that suspension of disbelief which the art-form demands—as people in their death-throes carol away for hours. After a splendid, rousing opening, Carmen entered. She was enormous, but enormous. She waddled about the stage in her corpulence, arch and inviting. She swept out, if she could be said to sweep anywhere and swept back in, twirling around Don Jose with an artificial carnation clenched between her teeth. She must have been the original Fat Lady. As soon as she appeared, I was convulsed by giggles. As the performance went on, they became uncontrollable. In the end I was heaving in and out of my seat in helpless laughter. I was asked to leave the theatre. Throughout the Occupation, I suspect I was the only Conqueror expelled from a theatre by the Conquered.

But life was proving pleasant with work, chess, German conversation and Rosa. There was one dreadful exception, feared by us all—the Werewolf. From time to time we were called out to the Cable Cellar a short distance away, generally at night. It was an underground warren of cables and connections which had survived although all the buildings at street level had been obliterated. You sallied out with a torch and some apparatus, made your way through two streets in pitch darkness, ruins all round, lit only by the fitful flicker of the torch. You reached a great door which came straight out of Dracula. It was heavy with huge iron studs, padlocks and chains. There was a massive knocker which you hammered—it always put me in mind of 'The servant boy to t'Palace came and knocked on the Ring.' There was deep stirring inside, much heavy breathing and panting, the rattle of chains, the clash of padlocks, and the door opened. He stood there, the Werewolf.

It was rumoured that he was a soldier wounded horribly on the Russian Front (where all bad things happened of course). He seemed huge and misshapen. He grunted and wheezed and barked. It was a time of the rumoured German Resistance, the Werewolves, of the Acht! Acht! heroes of Gottingen. You had to gain an entrance and make your way through what seemed miles of cellar, to find the fault, prop a ladder if need be and fix it, and then move back out, still in that ominous, flickering light. And with every step, there was this gigantic, snuffling menace at your shoulder. At the time, cigarettes were currency and I, mute, used to thrust a handful of them at him at the High Porte as I scuttled inside. Insurance.

But things went on fairly smoothly until May Day 1946. Suddenly the Station found itself surrounded by Red Flags. From every ruin, every half-standing building, from window crevices, from holes in the ground, Red Flags sprouted. They were rather peculiar Red Flags. They were long and narrow with a patch on the bottom where the swastikas used to be.

They were the work of the SED, the Socialist Unity Party. This sprang from the forced fusion of Socialists with the Communists in the Russian Zone which had strongholds in the West. Evidently Hannover Repeater Station was one.

We were seized by excitement. By that time, disgust with the Communists had taken me by the throat; that forced fusion I found repugnant. But however misguided, they were still comrades. Besides we owed them. Only a month or so earlier Bill Brown and I in a jeep had been caught in a food riot in the outskirts. It was a time when life was governed by the calorie level, forced lower and lower by Authority. Crowds ringed us, yelling curses, rocking the jeep and us with it, while, ironically as it turned out, we cursed ourselves for not having brought our rifles. Suddenly the crowd cleared, shunted to one side by SED stewards with red armbands who waved us through. So most of us rather revelled in the Red Flags. It was one in the eye for our masters, after all. We were rather pleased.

Not so our officer. He was a replacement for our usual man, just out from England. He came straight out of the bandbox, incredibly young, incredibly groomed, incredibly regimental. He was tiny, no bigger than I was and was very disciplinarian, at least in intention. He used expressions like 'Supernumerary Rank!' which invariably came out as 'Supernumewawy Wank!' Most of us had been in for three or four years, many of us had been through Normandy and we regarded him as a desperately unnecessary but unavoidable menace. We used to pray in public, High Church style, for his immediate departure.

Confronted with all those Red Flags, he ordered us to carry our loaded rifles into the Repeater Station. We had never done this before and we all thought it ludicrous. Most of the boys however shrugged it off, knowing it would last only a few days. Not so Muggins here. Was I a Soldier of the International or not? Misguided I may have considered the SED but they were still my comrades who had gone through travail Little Bo Peep from Sandhurst had never known. I was damned if I'd agree.

On parade the next morning I was not bearing my rifle at the High Porte. He ordered me to step aside. 'Sergeant Williams!' he barked. 'Do I understand that you are refusing to obey an order?' 'Yes, sir,' I replied with equal sonorousness, 'I consider the order stupid and unnecessary.' I had read the expression 'went puce': this was the first time I'd seen it. I was arrested on the spot, by two gigantic M.P.s. He must have had prior warning.

But where were they to put me? At first, delinquents used to spend a night or so in the town jail, but that was now filling up with displaced Poles, Frenchmen, Jugoslavs just like the good old days. It would never do now for a soldier of the British Army. Instead I was marched between the two giants into the school lavatory. They then discovered it was the girls' lavatory and I was ceremonially marched out to the boys'.

And there I stayed for days on end. I slept on a palliasse at night, was marched out when the boys went in for their ablutions, as the saying went, and back in when they'd gone. During the day I was permitted to wander a bit, always accompanied by a desperately bored M.P. In the end, he too learned chess and spiritually became One of Us.

Every morning, there was the same ritual. Supernumewawy Wank would stalk in, inflate himself to seven feet and proclaim . . . 'Sergeant Williams! Have you reconsidered your position?' I in turn would jack myself to eight feet, to retort—'No, sir, I have not!' And we'd glare at each other in utter intransigence across an impeccably masculine lavatory pan.

It went on for days until Higher Authority (rumour said it was General Brian Horrocks himself) sent down a note—'Turn the bugger loose and give him a Class B Release.' I never got the early Release.

The gang, who'd stopped carrying rifles days earlier, responded to my release in an unexpected manner. It would be too much to say I thought I should get a hero's welcome— but I thought I'd get appreciation for a stand on principle. Instead, in proper trade union manner, I was declared an un-person, boycotted, for a week. They were disgusted at my careless cruelty in landing them with my jobs over a triviality. Utterly morose, I did not see it that way at all.

And it was in that state of self-pitying disaffection that the Summons to the Werewolf came. In the usual state of dread, I lurched out of the Repeater Station, moved through the patch-work of light, dark and ruins to the Cable Cellar and, fighting down panic, hammered at the Ring. There was the usual clattering, groaning and muttering and the door swung open. The Werewolf stood there, breathing heavily. I, wordless, as usual, held up my handful of cigarettes. He did not move! He just stood there breathing in hoarse, retching gasps and at last he held out a huge paw. He was offering me a cigarette! He let out a snort which might have been a laugh and said . . . 'Come in! . . . Comrade!'

PEOPLE

I came into Merthyr station after demobilisation in 1947 in a state of anticipation. For years I had been Taffy, Taaf, Monsieur Taffy, Herr Taff, even Tovarich Taffy. Now, my own name at last! I had hardly taken five steps outside the station, when a man across the street bellowed—'Good Lord! It's Alf Gordon's grandson, isn't it?'

My grandfather Alfred Williams, from whom I got the middle name which has been the bane of my adult life, was universally known as Alf Gordon, apparently because of an alleged resemblance to General Gordon, who died at Khartoum, just a little south of where Sir Anthony Eden died, you'll remember. In Merthyr and Dowlais, I was known only by my grandfather's, my father's, even my brother's name. Sometimes I felt like the Invisible Man.

His own father was a pilot from Briton Ferry, who later kept the Tap Inn there. Whenever my father visited the place, he was hailed as one of the Taps. The pilot seems to have been a later Chartist who read the *People's Alfred*, a popular journal dedicated to the notion of Alfred as a 'people's king', which offered little consolation.

This pilot was alleged to have sent his son to something incomprehensible called a 'private school', but the Alfred Williams I knew was a collier working in the Bedlinog pits of the ubiquitous Dowlais Iron and Steel Company. He was a pillar of society except on Friday nights. My grandmother used to take me to the Antelope railway station in Dowlais Top, to greet the miners' train, commandeer his wage and make him an allowance.

I remember him as an enormously jovial man who never went near chapel. Known to the family as the General, he'd address me, eldest of the grandsons, as the Captain. 'Ah! my noble daughter-in-law!' he'd greet my mother, who doted on him, in an effort to cadge a little more drinking money. Widely respected, he was the first working man to be elected to the Board of Guardians under the old Poor Law. The whole of Dowlais used to see him off to meetings, resplendent in Sunday best, with an ornate waistcoat and gold watch-chain. He told me once that the proceedings of those meetings were in Welsh, even if the records were impeccably English—a salutary warning to historians!

He was a great Liberal who hated the new Labour Party. They cordially reciprocated and on election nights, a Labour crowd would gather around his big house in Ivor Terrace, overlooking Ivor Tip. If they'd won, they'd content themselves with the Red Flag. But if they'd lost, they'd try to break the door in. My grandfather and his sons would stand by with pick-axe handles in the passage. Since those sons had by then joined the Labour Party, this afforded me an early introduction to the Marxist notion of the Dialectic!

My grandfather died of cancer. He was in such pain that he tore the mantelpiece from the wall. At his funeral, I remember hundreds upon hundreds of booted feet shuffling through Dowlais.

His wife, my grandmother Mary Catherine Hughes, was tiny, no more than five foot and nearly always dressed in black. I convinced myself in my youth that she had built Gwernllwyn Chapel with her bare teeth. Whenever she saw me reading a newspaper, she'd bear down on me. 'What's the worrld to you, boy?' she'd cry, tearing the offending *News Chronicle* from my grasp, '*Cere at dy* Literature', (Get down to your Literature).

Education was her grand passion. She had two objectives for me—Higher, the equivalent of A level, and Aberr—Aberystwyth University College, to us almost a mythical institution. There were only two kinds of job worth having, she said. You worked with your hands which was at least honest or else it was 'Teacherr, Doctorr or Preacherr'. I achieved the first of her ambitions, could be said to have obtained the second; according to some, I collared the lot!

She was a Gog, as North Walians came to be called among us. There was a family legend that her father had taken the whole clan on foot from Mynydd Parys, Amlwch in Anglesey all the way to Dowlais. She maintained her connections with the Hugheses, which was why my father went to Bangor Normal training college for teachers, another mythical institution. Packed with South Walians, it was then much less of a parochial institution than its neighbour, Bangor University College. In the long series of Varsity v. College rugby matches, the University never won a game for twenty years. My father got both his rugby and his soccer cap at the Normal.

This meant that T. Rowland Hughes, the celebrated novelist in Welsh, became a Welsh uncle. His books were compulsory reading in our house. My grandmother supported him, particularly after his move south into real poverty before he landed his job with the BBC. The fate of his bookcase was later a cause of some fraternal rivalry. She subsidised half of Gwernllwyn Chapel anyway; she was a pillar of the place.

She was the real sinew of the family, running a bakeshop and laundry in Ivor Street before they moved to Ivor Terrace (Ivor was the name of Lady Charlotte Guest's favourite son). Her own children and the multitudinous offspring of her many kinsfolk all became schoolteachers; my own immediate family were over-whelmingly a teacher family. In my youth I was cocooned in a vast cousinage dedicated to education. I used to claim I could spot a teacher at a hundred yards; when I was wrong, it was a member of that lost breed, an H.M.I.

In truth, she had a real sense of humour, on display every Sunday when we went there for dinner. Although she used regularly to denounce my mother for carelessness, she appreciated her company. She once stormed into Gwernllwyn chapel to denounce '*Yr hen Mussolini 'na,*' which convulsed the congregation. Towards the end, she had an accident and became a little odd. Working for my Higher, I used to spend many hours in her house, with its large and freezing walk-in larder and its tiny front study, reserved for me. Ostensibly I was looking after her, while her daughter was at work. She once came up and pressed a half-crown into my hand. To queries she replied—'The poor dab looks as if he could do with half a crown.' She died just after I went into the Army in November 1943.

My mother's family were much more romantic, at least in her

estimation. Her then-dead but cherished father was, according to her—'all red and rosy, a real countryman.' John Morgan came from Cil-y-Cwm in Carmarthenshire. There was a Scottish presence there, usually bailiffs, and my mother endowed him with a distinguished Scottish ancestry. We'd spend hours of an evening, poring over books of kilts to choose our own! We settled in the end on the Lovatts. The truth came out much later. He was the illegitimate son of a man called Vipond, whose Vipond's Drift was a feature of Cil-y-Cwm. He fathered him on a local girl and farmed him out to a family called Morgan. Up to Dowlais and the pits he came, with several brothers and cousins, as West Walian as you can get. Unlike the rest of us, he was an Anglican and a Tory. He refused to vote for Keir Hardie, even when his daughters threatened to cut off his tobacco. '*Beth? Yr hen Scotchie 'na? Na, na, Foxe-Davies a Rector bech i mi!* What? That old Scotsman? No, no, Foxe-Davies (the Tory candidate) and the little Rector for me!' 'Tory I am,' he'd declare, 'Me firrst firrst, you firrst after!' Which on reflection isn't a bad description of Thatcherism!

Far more respectable to us was my mother's maternal kin. They were Herberts, a radical family of ironmongers and general merchants from Abergavenny and the Monmouthshire valleys who, I later discovered, had been important in the early nineteenth-century history of Merthyr; in fact they dominated my book on the town. They were Unitarians, a striking and radical denomination who were key players in the politics of early nineteenth-century Britain. They certainly were in Merthyr, taking local power at the time of the Merthyr Rising of 1831 and sharing it with the Guests. One was the first to introduce Cobbett and other radical writers to the Valleys, another was an M.P.

This wasn't enough for Mam who made them descendants, under the blanket, of the aristocratic Herberts of Raglan Castle and God knows where else! She claimed her family . . . 'spent pounds, POUNDS they spent' . . . trying to find a crucial document which would have got a lost estate out of Chancery. This, it seems, would have given us ground rents in Talgarth, Upper Chapel Farm, Breconshire and the whole of Llangorse

Lake! What we'd have done with Llangorse Lake I can't think—though having filmed Avalon for the TV programmes *Excalibur* there, we might have got a facility fee!

The real heroine was her grandmother, Sarah Herbert, who married three times and exercised moral control over Dowlais from her shop in Penywern. Once she took my mother in tow to Dowlais market where a huckster was displaying what he alleged was the ear of Dic Penderyn, the 'martyr' of the Merthyr Rising. She soon put a stop to such goings-on.

She became the election agent in Dowlais of Henry Richard, 'The Apostle of Peace' who won a famous victory for democracy in the Merthyr election of 1868. Her brother Roger was a later Chartist who subscribed to and wrote for the *Merthyr Star*. He used to run a Chartist Sunday School in Nant-y-Glo. There he taught *Volney's Ruins*, gobbets and all, a celebrated text from the French Revolution which had a great influence on working-class radicals and was translated very early into Welsh. It was a key text in Mary Shelley's *Frankenstein!* When I heard that his papers had survived among his descendants, I hared over to Monmouthshire only to be told by a cousin—'Oh! those old Chartist papers and things? Burned them ages ago.' I felt a spasm of murderous rage. It's hard to be a historian among a people which is increasingly losing its grip on its own past.

My mother was the only one in her family to succumb to our hereditary disease and become a schoolteacher. She was trained in Portsmouth College in the last years of World War I. She thoroughly enjoyed it. On Armistice Night, the students were allowed out, provided they were roped together and were back by 7 p.m.! All those sailors, I suppose. Mam used to carol 'Play up Pompey!' at the least excuse and we spent three summer holidays on the eve of World War II in Southsea.

I loved Southsea, the smell of early morning bacon in our digs, the Prom, the beaches, the theatres. We saw 'The White Horse Inn' there, the first colour movie and 'Things to Come'—which entranced me. War was imminent and the night sky was laced by searchlights, with a plane occasionally caught in them. We went religiously to Navy Week in Portsmouth, to see the *Victory* and dramatic displays. We once saw the cruiser *Aurora* beat off an aerial attack—which she was to do in reality in the Med a few years later. There I swam all the way from South Marine Pier to Clarence Pier—which came to loom in my mind like an epic. I went back years later and found to my surprise that it really had been! I could never do it now.

The Prom of an evening was a sight—tense and crowded meetings, Communist and Fascist on the Spanish Civil War which then filled our imagination—and dwarfing them all, the huge gathering around the Salvation Army band. The owner of our digs, who became a family friend, used to bang the big drum in that band. His daughter was the only fly in the ointment.

She, much older than I, was allotted me to 'look after' on some afternoons. She would take me to a park for some erotic and cheap thrill. I used to lie there, with her blouse off, sweating in frustrated misery, as my fingers encountered knicker elastic . . . 'I can't get any lower'. She sat bolt upright, slammed me across the face and snapped 'I don't want you to get any lower!' In later years I was to recollect the experience in acute frustration, and at the time it was sheer hell. I used to devise urgent needs to rush down to the beach, on my own. No wonder I scored that remarkable swim. Frustration was my fuel.

My mother's three brothers were all colliers invalided out of the pits because of their chests. Uncle Dafydd, a small neat, twinkling man, spent a happy retirement supported by his children, but was reduced to hours of silence by his large indefatigably talkative wife. When she died, he erected a tombstone in defiance of all criticism—*Fe ddaeth ddistawrwydd mawr*, there came a great silence!

Unlce Johnny, a brilliant pianist, found a place as a church organist in North Molton, Devon where he is commemorated by a plaque. The place was governed, benevolently as a whole, by an aristocratic family. His lively wife ran the village school where I went during holidays. I enjoyed the place with a genuine country feel to it, watching my cousin develop his photographs, an art to which I was introduced, and revelling in its walks. We followed a stag hunt once, right through to the sickening kill, with Dad stalking among horses and dogs, muttering into his pipe about feudalism.

He never changed his routine, going out for a drink in the evening and chatting away with a neighbour even though he confessed he never understood a word! More feudalism. Though indeed, in the school, I found the kids much more backward than they were in Merthyr and Dowlais. Trained for their place in life, I expect; Dad was right.

Uncle Will was a character, full of humour, teasing, half-baked memories, full of bilingual strike songs and much other folklore, which completely defeated a BBC team I once brought in to record him. He used to hope for the odd tip from my mother and we all enjoyed his delightful wife and daughter. He was a great hit in the many Whist Drives he organised. My father remained utterly suspicious of him, leaving the house as soon as he entered. Strange really, because Uncle Will used to run an insurance book which, at election times, he'd make over to the Labour Party—to my mother's intense rage.

I now realise my mother's family stemmed from a quite different political tradition from my father's who followed a normal south Wales route out of Liberalism into the Labour Party. Out of respect for his own father and an ever-diminishing commitment to Lloyd George, my father only joined the Labour Party in its disastrous electoral year of 1931. (Whenever a Williams joined a cause, it was doomed!) Once there, he swiftly turned our house into a teeming warren of a ward office and himself into a local hero and a great friend of our MP, S. O. Davie, a flamboyant and leftwing orator who always dressed in virtually Edwardian style. My mother denounced S. O. as a traitor to the I.L.P.

Her family had moved from Henry Richard and Chartists into the most radical variant of socialism available, bar the communists who were beyond the pale. Those three brothers of hers were swept up in the Revival of 1904. This didn't last, but they remained teetotallers all their lives and moved into the scarcely less evangelical fervour of the Independent Labour Party of Keir Hardie who used to open their hillside with a hymn.

My mother's elder sister married Evan Morgan, an I.L.P. stalwart who left the pits to graduate from the School of Mines as a health and safety inspector and to achieve the virtually unique distinction of being blacklisted by both Powell Duffryn, the coal-owners and the Fed, the South Wales Miners' Federation. In the end, he had to emigrate and his family spent poverty-stricken years in camps. He ended his days as Chief Inspector of Mines in the State of Alberta, Canada—an early source of the endless American comics which brightened my youth.

'Dic Wallhead was the best M.O. Merthyr ever had!' my mother would declaim in the turbulent sixties, citing an obscure I.L.P. man from the early days—at a time when Labour was at grips with Plaid Cymru. She harassed my father with a guerilla war over meals, as he was simultaneously wrestling with Plaid and with a dissident I.L.P. teacher who threatened his headship. Her ILP-ism however, sat very uneasily with her occasional prolonged outbursts of a prurient royalism and a tribal Welsh nationalism—not to mention her ingrained petty-bourgeois snobbery—which most times she recognised herself.

I realise fully now that my parents lived in different worlds. After early clashes and as the family grew older, the evenings tended to be strained. Mam would hold court, but over my strongly disputed marriage to a girl of Spanish descent, she'd subject me to a merciless campaign of intimidation, though indulging my younger brother. My father, returning from a night of much-cherished argument in his favourite pub, would slump in his chair, fiddling with radio and his pipe, his mouth moving in endless debate with some-one, sometimes exploding in utterly incomprehensible comment, until it was time for a terse good-night. During Dad's last illness they grew close, but for much of the time I think Mam was unhappy. She should never have been a housewife—even a headmaster's wife—in macho south Wales.

She was, for example, an actress born. She had genuine gifts—but never, never would she display them before my father, partly from a weird kind of respect for him, partly from fear at being mocked and dismissed. His own brother, the playwright, used to drive himself crazy trying to lure her into his drama groups. But everyone else, our juvenile gang in the kitchen, the Sisterhood, charabanc trips, groups of friends she would convulse, even, astonishing though it now seems, over racy stories!

Her great days came, I imagine, when the BBC sponsored a comedienne of the same name—Gwladys Morgan. There were endless calls for Mam to perform. One I particularly remember. The husband of the BBC's Gwladys had to bale out of a stricken aircraft over Aberystwyth on a Sunday—'but, as you know, nothing ever opens in Aber on a Sunday'—Mam told it better.

The jewel in the crown was a story about a family trip to a posh restaurant in Cardiff; Mam replendent over the crockery, little finger raised over a coffee cup, snobbery on full display. Then a Valleys voice from over the way—'Gwladys! Gwladys!'—and my mother's agonies of embarrassment as she tried to ignore her. It was an unduly prolonged epic in which Mam played all the parts: herself, Valleys friend, customers, oily waiter and irate *maitre d'hotel*—no wonder she was fond of Kenneth Griffith!

There was a bite to the performance. On the rare occasions the family did go down to Cardiff for a special meal, my father had a habit of suddenly leaning forward and calling to a waitress— 'WHERE is the URINAL?' presumably to watch Mam swoon away into social death! We were then a little edgy about Cardiff, even Christmas Cardiff. Mam used to recall that she'd approach the posh shops and their even posher assistants, cultivating an 'English' accent and apologetically suppressing her Welsh— whereas in her maturity, she'd march up to the counter and address them in a loud and self-confident Welsh—to watch them squirm in apology.

I suppose her theatrical gifts helped make her a brilliant teacher. That she was, particularly with younger kids. She thoroughly enjoyed teaching (more stories!) before slumping into what she felt was the slow death of married life with its fixed rituals for women. She was delighted when she went back during the war and was very reluctant indeed to give it up again.

This was, for me, the first hint I got of contradictions both within herself and with my father. I went to school very early, long before the 'official' time. Dowlais Central with its attendant Infants' had originally been Lady Charlotte Guest's foundation and still enjoyed some prestige. My aunt Rachel, Dad's sister, dominated the Infant's. Dad performed in the Central.

For five years my teacher was my father. Since he was a very good teacher, I obviously derived great benefit. I was literate and numerate, I devoured books, always in abundant supply, journals—anything Dad favoured. But it was (or must have been, since I was only half-conscious of such things) a strain. Dad was monumentally fair. The stick was commonplace. If I were caught in an offence for which other kids got one cut, I got two. The first time it happened, I boasted of it to Mam—a kind of rite of passage after all! She immediately tore into Dad who promptly denounced me as a sneak. An early lesson in the necessary hypocrisy of social intercourse.

When I and an equally tiny friend were later repeatedly bullied on our way home, not a word crossed my lips. Instead, there was an epic fight in Dowlais yard when my pal withdrew almost at once and I was left facing up to this great thug for hours on end, until opinion among the crowd shifted in my favour and it stopped. So did the bullying.

But there was a lot to bear. On no account was I to call Dad 'Sir' at the supper table, nor, of course 'Dad' at school. I must always remember that I was a teacher's son and behave accordingly. This proved much more difficult than you might expect. I date my stammer from this period—made worse by Aunt Rachel's remorselessly sustained attempts to cure me (she was also something of a *ffyrnig*, fierce evangelical and had herself suffered from stammering). I was put out to a teacher for piano lessons, my aunt Rachel was an ardent lieutenant and when, after quite a successful career through the Trinity College of Music examinations, I finally invented an illness and bunked it, she was present at the post-mortem with Dad and the piano teacher when I was finally let off.

Throughout all this, Mam who 'vamped' and claimed to know only one key, used to play endlessly in the front room of a Sunday evening, with me curled at her feet in rapt enjoyment. Her versions of 'Poor Old Joe' with its repeated dissolve into tears became famous. I remembering being struck in later years, reading F. R. Leavis's defence of D. H. Lawrence and the Nonconformist tradition against T. S. Eliot, when 'the boom of the tingling strings' figured in an identical scene from Lawrence's own youth.

Editorial Note

Gwyn wrote the first stories in this collection while he was undergoing his first chemotherapy treatment. The thought of not writing, even under those circumstances, was anathema to him. He decided on the autobiographical stories since they would be easier and not involve any research. They were also a preparation for the programme that he had agreed to record in January 1995. His progress was erratic but he managed to write most of the stories in this book: they were tales that he had polished over the years—usually to an appreciative audience—in public and private. These reminiscences obviously led him to think more deeply about his childhood and the people that he knew in Merthyr, especially his family. Under the circumstances, these were not lighthearted anecdotes of events that were safely tucked away in the past. Gwyn in common, I suspect, with many men of his generation was uncomfortable with emotions that he was forcing himself to acknowledge almost for the first time. He was not happy with this work and was reluctant to carry on with it. His illness progresed rapidly in the last few months and he had no energy to complete this last chapter, although he worried about it almost until the end of his life. However, it has been included in this volume—it seems to me a fitting, if incomplete, conclusion to his autobiography writing.

SIÂN LLOYD.